IT CAN
BE DONE

The Billy Henderson Story

To: Matthew Finn

Best wishes!

Ed Grisamore

by Ed Grisamore

Henchard Press Ltd.

Publisher	Henry S. Beers
Associate Publisher	Richard J. Hutto
Executive Vice President	Robert G. Aldrich
Operations Manager	Gary G. Pulliam
Editor-in-Chief	Joni Woolf
Art Director/Designer	Julianne Gleaton
Designer	Daniel Emerson
Director of Marketing and Public Relations	Mary D. Robinson

Printed in the USA.

Library of Congress Control Number: 2005932294

ISBN: (13 digit) 978-0-9770912-1-8
(10 digit) 0-9770912-1-X

Henchard Press Ltd. books are available at quantity discounts with bulk purchase for educational, business, or sales promotional use. For information, please write to:
Henchard Press Ltd., 3920 Ridge Avenue, Macon, GA 31210, or call 866-311-9578.

To My Family: Fosky, Brad, Fran, Carol, Johnny and Chris,
and to the memory of my mother, Jewell Henderson.
They all helped make me who I am.

TABLE OF CONTENTS

FOREWORD

I never had the privilege of playing football for Billy Henderson.

I never got to hear his motivational speeches in the sweat of the locker room. I never got to follow the snap of his voice, demanding and loving wrapped in the same breath. I never had him extract every ounce of energy from my muscles, and then go back for more.

"Grisamore!" I can hear him screaming on my imaginary football field, "I need eight more pints of sweat!"

I regret that time and geography didn't allow me a spot on one of his rosters. He probably wouldn't have had much use for a skinny tight end. But I have no doubts he would have made me a better player and – more importantly – a better person.

I say this because I have met hundreds of his former players. They come from all walks of life and all levels of playing ability. They now range in age from their late 20s to one of the oldest, who just turned 70.

The generations can swap stories from the same war chest. The newspaper clippings preserved between the pages of the scrapbook have faded. The lessons learned between those pages have not.

Although I never played a down of football for Coach Henderson, in many ways I feel like I did.

After all, what is a coach but a teacher? He has never stopped teaching, even folks like me.

The first time I heard of Billy Henderson was in a column by Lewis Grizzard in 1977. He said Henderson had the "last crew cut in captivity." Of course, my impression from a distance was that the man was hard-nosed and old-fashioned. Over time, what I've come to realize is that the only thing wrong with Billy Henderson is there aren't enough coaches like him.

I've absorbed a lifetime of lessons in the 25 years since I first introduced myself, shaking his firm hand at a high school football game in Macon in 1979. The game was played at Brad Henderson Memorial Stadium, which was named after Billy's late son.

Even from a distance, I have absorbed his wisdom, marveled at his organizational skills and been profoundly moved by this journey of sharing the joys and sorrows of his remarkable life.

On a side note, I credit Coach Henderson for making me a morning person.

In 1996, I interviewed him for a story for The Macon Telegraph. He told me he arrived at his office at Clarke Central every day at 5 a.m. Long before the janitors even got to the school, he studied game film, took notes and organized the day's practice schedule.

After I interviewed him, I remember waking up early the next morning and looking at the clock. It was 5 a.m.

"I'm lying here in bed," I thought, "and Coach Henderson is already hard at work."

So I got up. Gradually, I began to discipline myself to arise each day at 5 a.m. Soon, I began to savor that time of the day. It was my time. To this day, it is still my routine.

Of course, much of my admiration for Coach Henderson is embedded in the testimonies of those who have lived alongside him – his family and friends. I could include his players, too, but they are one in the same as family and friends.

In October 2004, Coach Henderson asked me to write this book. Words are how I make my living. But, in this case, I was honored beyond words.

I will always cherish the time we spent working together on this project. We spent many hours at his "office" at the Holiday Inn in Athens and the den of his home, where there are so many photographs and memories of his playing and coaching days they cover the walls of his carport, too.

I continue to be amazed at the people who not only know him, but still call him "Coach." I'm convinced there are only two people in Athens who always can answer to that honorable title. They are Vince Dooley and Billy Henderson.

It has been not so much of a project but a pilgrimage. It has given me rich insight and even greater admiration for one of America's greatest high school coaches, a man who still sings "The Impossible Dream" from "Man of La Mancha" in the shower every morning.

More importantly, it gave Coach Henderson, at age 77, a chance to re-examine his life – the triumphs and the heartaches. Reflection can be a wonderful thing, full of both joys and regrets.

I am thankful for his willingness to share. His is a story that needed to be told. And, as the saying goes, none of us should die with the music inside us.

On June 15, 2005, a few months before the publication of this book, he wrote me a note of gratitude for helping him tell his story.

"You have taken me on a 77-year journey, and it has been exciting every step of the way," he wrote. "I should pay you for being my shrink. I have learned so much and understand more vividly what and who I am. Thanks!"

No, coach. Thank you.

The honor is mine.

Ed Grisamore
Macon, Ga.
October 2005

A young Billy Henderson plays at a Macon park in the 1930s.
(Photo courtesy of Henderson family.)

THE GIFT

There are moments that change our lives forever.

They are the blackboards that teach us. They are the compasses we keep in our pockets. They are the stars that guide us in the night sky.

For Billy Henderson, that moment came on Sept. 17, 1941, when he climbed the steps of Lanier High School.

He had passed this school thousands of times growing up in Macon, Ga., watching the high school boys walk to class in their military uniforms.

Now it was his turn. He was 13 years old, a young man with boundless energy and spirit. He had an idea of what high school would be like for him. But he had no way of knowing the impact of what awaited him inside those doors, where 1,600 other boys grew into men on ROTC fields, and in the sweat and tears of locker rooms.

On that first day of classes in 1941, he checked his schedule on the large bulletin board in the front hallway. There weren't many options. Students couldn't drop classes, request teachers or rearrange their schedules to suit their own needs. You got what was given to you, and you accepted it.

Billy Henderson went to the gymnasium and there it was – in letters and words larger than life. On the wall were the words:

"WE LEAD."

"IT CAN BE DONE."

Those would be words he would take with him. They would shape his world as he would lead others. They would define him. They would encourage him. No matter how difficult the challenge or how heavy the grief he had to bear, they stuck to his heart and never wobbled.

"IT CAN BE DONE."

His oath of commitment. His theme song. A tattoo on his soul.

He came into the world as William Bradford Henderson on June 2, 1928, on the edge of the Great Depression. He was born in Dublin, Ga., the youngest of four children born to Holly Bradford Henderson and Mina Jewell Henderson. He had two older sisters, Kathryn and Doris, and an older brother, James. Folks called James "Red," the same nickname they called his daddy.

Red Henderson worked for the railroad when he met Jewell Fouche. She was one of 11 children who grew up on a cotton farm near Sylvester, Ga. He was from Tennille. He was 21. She was 15. They took their own rail car down the tracks from Sandersville the day they married.

In the early years of their marriage, Red got jobs as a master mechanic all over the Southeast. After Billy was born in Dublin, the family moved to Macon and then Savannah before returning to Dublin when Billy was in the third grade.

It was living on South Lawrence Street in Dublin where Billy forged the strongest memories of his father. Red Henderson took great pride in everything he did.

"Even though he was a mechanic, he always wore a coat and tie to work," said Henderson. "He would change when he got there. He would work all day, then take a shower and put back on his coat and tie and walk home. We didn't have a car, so he had to walk everywhere."

Red Henderson was also an outgoing person who never met a stranger. He had a soft spot in his heart for people who were down on their luck.

"My mother never knew who he was going to bring home to live with us," said Henderson. "Sometimes it was a relative. Sometimes it was a friend."

But, in the eyes of his youngest son, Red Henderson possessed another quality that towered above his pride in his appearance and compassion for others.

He was a great athlete.

"He was 6-foot-1 without an ounce of fat on him," said Henderson. "I always remember my daddy racing all the other men on South Lawrence Street. He was fast. He could outrun every one of them. I would go and watch him play baseball and softball. I taught myself to bat left-handed because of him."

Billy was one month shy of his ninth birthday when Red Henderson died in May 1937. He had appendicitis and refused to go to the doctor. He stayed on the sofa. His appendix erupted and gangrene set in.

A lot of people came to the house when he died.

"I don't remember the funeral," said Henderson.

What he does remember was the tremendous void it left in his life, a hole his mother and others would step in to fill.

If Billy Henderson has had one hero in his life, it was his mother.

"Her joy was providing for her children," he said. "She never complained. She was 37 years old when my father died. She was a beautiful young widow. People tried to get her interested in other men but she wouldn't have any part of it. She was a one-man woman for life. She gave me an unrealistic view of life. To this day, I still think all women are virtuous."

His sisters, Kathryn and Doris, were married and lived in Macon. So Jewell Henderson moved James and Billy with her to Macon, where they first lived with Kathryn, then Doris. Kathryn was married to Sam Dinardo, a Yankee she met when he was stationed with the Army at nearby Camp Wheeler.

Jewell Henderson found jobs wherever she could. She worked as a nurse in home health care. She worked in the nursery at Pendleton Homes. There was never much money, but you would never know it. She gave her boys the things money couldn't buy.

"We thought we were wealthy," said Henderson. "We had everything we needed. I knew there was somebody in this world who loved me, and I wanted to please her. Her whole life was her family.

"No matter how bad things got, we were always clean and neat," he said. "We had a clean shirt every day. We qualified for the welfare lunch program, but my mother would have no part of that. Every day, she would pack us a sack lunch with a peanut butter and cracker sandwich."

There was no heat in the home. At bedtime on winter nights, Billy and James would get warm by the coal fire place, then sprint to the bedroom and get under the covers.

She also taught her two sons Bible verses. They would watch her read and recite scripture. And she lived her life according to the Good Book.

"She set the highest example," he said. "I would rather see than hear a sermon any day."

Henderson started fourth grade at Gresham Elementary that next fall, where he came under the influence of several teachers who gave him the encouragement he needed as a young boy living in a single-parent home.

There was Miss Respress in the fourth grade, and Miss Kendall in the fifth. He remembers winning the broad jump in a track meet the Macon Recreation Department held one weekend. The next Monday in class, Miss Kendall stood in front of the students and walked off the distance of 13 feet, 6 inches.

"Now this, class," she said, "is how far Billy jumped in the broad jump."

Like any child, Billy craved the attention. It wasn't long before he would realize he had been given a gift.

"God gave me athletic ability," he said. "It would open doors for me."

Other teachers helped him find his way. In the sixth grade, Miss Weiss taught him about architecture and the world. It fascinated him. In the seventh grade, Miss Mullenix was a very strict teacher. But when they went on the playground at recess, she was a different person. She would play softball with them.

School was not his only classroom. The Henderson family lived with Kathryn and Sam in a little house on Columbus Street.

"My whole world was Columbus Street," said Henderson.

There was a small park by the railroad tracks. A large city park, Tattnall Square, was just a block away, and the campus of Mercer University was nearby. A pair of roller skates would take you all over the city.

He would play follow the leader with his friends, dodging the cars up and down College Street. Some of his best friends in the neighborhood were Wallace Criswell, Parks Creech, Arthur "Brother" Schmidt, Cleve Swisher, Charles Edmonds, Paul Smith and Billy Kitchens.

The house had a back porch, where he and his buddy, Arthur Schmidt, would trade baseball cards. In the side yard, they would mimic Rabbit Garrett, who played for the Macon Peaches, by throwing the baseball over their heads and catching it.

He loved Garrett and Eddie Stanky, who fashioned himself in the same firebrand mold as Ty Cobb. Stanky couldn't hit or field much but he was filled to the brim with desire. (He later made it to the major leagues as a manager.)

"The so-called experts said he couldn't run, he couldn't hit and he couldn't throw," said Henderson. "It's a good thing he didn't listen to those experts."

The Peaches were Macon's minor-league baseball team and were steeped in tradition. They played their games at Luther Williams Field, which was built in 1929 and remains one of the oldest minor-league ballparks in the country.

He had no extra money to attend the games, so he would walk the three miles from his house and stand outside the stadium with the rest of the knot-hole gang. They would wait for foul balls outside the grandstand. Returning a retrieved foul ball would get you free admission to the game.

"Whenever a foul ball came over, we looked like flushed quail," he said. "That's where I learned to run fast. It was very competitive. You had to be aggressive. Sometimes you had to fight for the ball."

He developed his athletic skills on the dusty sandlots of Macon. There were few rules and, of course, a few provisions. The neighborhood headquarters was at the home of Claude Lewis. (Lewis would later become the longtime director of the Warner Robins Recreation Department and is widely regarded as the "Father of T-Ball.")

"If you had a bat, you could play. And, if you had a glove, you had it made," said Henderson. The catcher rarely wore a mask. They didn't have one.

"The games would last until somebody broke a window," he said, laughing.

He often found himself playing against older boys. Although he was smaller, he could hold his own.

He also became involved in organized sports through the Macon Recreation Department and local Boys Club. He played for the North Highland Skull Busters and the West Macon Giants. Mrs. Beggs was the recreation director, and would drive through the neighborhoods to meet with the boys.

"We were always glad to see her car," said Billy. "It was always filled with bats and balls."

Times were still hard for his family. He was the only player on the team without a uniform. One day, his mother got off work and took him with her. They went in several downtown stores looking for a business that would sponsor him by providing him a uniform.

"I learned some new words that day," he said. "We can't accommodate you. It's not in our budget. She really felt bad about it. And I said, 'Don't worry about it, Mama.'"

In the summer of 1940, the West Macon Giants played East Macon for the age 12-and-under city championship at Luther Williams Field. Henderson won't ever forget it. It would provide an early lesson in sportsmanship. After 16 innings, the game was tied 2-2. Beggs declared co-champions, and the teams got together and cut watermelons.

He grew up at First Street Methodist and was baptized at age 11. The minister had gone around to all the Sunday School rooms and asked if anyone wanted to be baptized. Henderson raised his hand.

If his mother was his hero, Louie Wanninger was his kindred spirit. He was 11 years old when he met Louie at the Boys Club on Cotton Avenue in the summer of 1939.

"That was my outlet after school," said Henderson. "I would go there to play basketball and shoot pool. I looked up one day and Louie was standing in the doorway. He was wearing a sailor's cap and leaning on one hand. He had this aura about him. He was self-confident, and he backed it up.

"He grabbed a cue stick. He didn't ask us to play. He just came in. He looked like he owned the place."

He took his shot and the balls vanished into the pockets. It was that way with Louie. He had the magic touch.

Louie's father was Pee Wee Wanninger, a former teammate of Babe Ruth with the 1925 New York Yankees. It was Lou Gehrig who pinch hit for Wanninger in the eighth inning against the Washington Senators on June 1, 1925. Gehrig then replaced Wally Pipp at first base to begin his streak of 2,130 consecutive games.

Billy and Louie became the best of friends. If you saw one, you saw the other. He was perhaps the most unforgettable character of Henderson's life.

"We were like Tom Sawyer and Huck Finn," said Billy. "He had a dominant personality. In a room full of 500 people, he would be the one talking. He was likeable, interesting and fresh. I would jump in the fire with him. It was a long time before I knew I could make a decision on my own."

Said Wanninger: "Billy had a shock of jet black hair that bounced when he ran, pearly white teeth and very long legs. He didn't look the part at 12 years old, but we soon realized we were watching an exceptional athlete."

They used to race to the drug store on College Hill. Louie would call Billy on the telephone, and they would dash out the door to see who arrived there first.

"He started beating me every time," said Henderson. "It was years before I found out he was calling me from the drug store."

They once cut classes at school to go swimming in the Ocmulgee River – in the dead of winter. The current was too strong, and the water was freezing.

"But Louie had a solution for everything," Henderson said. "For some reason, we covered ourselves in sand."

There was also the time when an irate owner of a pecan tree on New Street caught the two trespassing. He grabbed Henderson's arm and asked him his name.

"Billy Henderson, 330 Columbus Street."

When the man asked Louie the same question, came the reply:

"Al Capone, Chicago, Ill."

Louie and Billy went through the backfield of boyhood together. On the football teams at the Boys Club, Louie always played right halfback, and Billy was always left halfback.

(Henderson remembers a game years later, when the two were in the same high school backfield. Every time Louie would return to the huddle he would say, "Let's win this one for Charley!" Finally, Billy said to him: "Louie, we don't even have a Charley!" As it turned out, Louie was nursing a charley horse.)

He may have been a free spirit. But Louie Wanninger taught Billy Henderson something in the years before his teachers, coaches and classmates at Lanier began to wield their enormous influence on his life. (He died in August 2000 but, in Henderson's words, he still lives inside him.)

It Can Be Done.

On Sept. 17, 1941, a young man walked up the steps to Lanier High School.

"Little did I know what was waiting for me inside that school," he said.

Henderson, left, beats friend Louie Wanninger at the wire for Lanier High School in a track meet at Porter Stadium. Wanninger later joked he was distracted by a beautiful young lady as the two crossed the finish line. (Photo courtesy of Henderson family.)

THE MACON METEOR

Never once did he try to compare himself to any of the other 1,600 young men at Lanier. Some came from affluent families. Their fathers were attorneys, doctors and city councilmen.

Lanier was the great equalizer.

"I didn't have to compare myself to them," he said. "We all had uniforms. You couldn't tell one person from another."

Roger "Red" Wilson, his teammate and friend, looked around and saw the same kind of equality.

"It didn't matter if you were rich or poor, you were all in the same boat," said Wilson. "It didn't matter who your parents were or how much money you had. Those wool uniforms scratched everybody."

But Henderson began to separate himself from some of the other eighth-grade athletes who were being indoctrinated into the world of high school athletics.

It was the beginning of a high school career that would put him in the ranks as one of the greatest athletes in Macon prep sports history, a two-time All-American in both football and baseball.

"Lanier was the finest high school known to man," Henderson said. "We would walk up those steps, and they didn't give us any choices. If you happened to be a slow student, buddy, you learned to keep up with the fast ones. There was pride and togetherness. There were no union-card holders."

The Lanier Poets got their nickname from their namesake, Sidney Lanier, one of the most famous poets of the 19th century and a native of Macon. It wasn't the most masculine of nicknames, and Lanier was often teased by opponents. But the Poets proved themselves in the sports arena as one of the top programs in Georgia high school athletics.

During his first fall on campus, Henderson was in a group of junior varsity athletes identified by football coach John "Stooge" Davis as being potential rising stars in the program. The idea was to move them up to the varsity ahead of schedule. They would provide the nucleus for a future championship team. Among the others were Wanninger, Wilson, Carl "Bulldog" Hudson, James Dean, Alton Dean, George Wright and Gardner Dickinson, who later became a star on the PGA tour.

All became involved in an after-school, touch football program under the supervision of Davis. An upperclassman, Bill Kent, coached the squad.

Sure, the girls were beginning to catch his eye. But Henderson's true love was sports. Over the next four years, he would earn 14 letters in football, basketball, baseball and track. That's more than half the alphabet.

For everything, there was a season.

"If they had soccer, I would have played that, too," he said.

"He was a special athlete," said friend Claude Lewis. "We knew back then he was a step above the rest of us and would go on to play in college and professionally."

Said Wilson: "I never saw him give anything less than 100 percent every time he was on the field."

Henderson, along with his teammates, was the beneficiary of perhaps the greatest assembly of coaches in the history of Macon high school sports.

There was Davis, Tom Porter, Cotton Harrison, H.P. Bell and Lem Clark. Their sphere of influence went far beyond the locker rooms and playing fields.

"They had all the qualities that later helped shape me as a coach," said Henderson. "They took an interest in every player as a person."

Davis took a little too much interest in Henderson one morning before school, when he found him and another boy involved in a game of shooting dice at the base of the steps to the high school.

He marched them to the principal's office, where they got a long lecture from Principal L.W. Lewis. They were given a choice of 10 licks with a paddle or 10 days suspension.

"I went first and said I would take the 10 licks," said Henderson. "I reached down and grabbed my ankles. Coach Davis was giving the licks. On the fifth one, the paddle broke.

"The other guy changed his mind. He said he would take the suspension."

His impact in athletics, especially on the football field, came quickly. As a ninth grader, he played in his first game against Atlanta's Commercial High School at Porter Stadium in Macon. He scored four touchdowns as a tailback lined up in the Notre Dame box.

He certainly wasn't the most physically imposing player on the field. He was 5-foot-8 and weighed 130 pounds.

His speed was what separated him from the rest of the pack. (In college, he would pick up the nickname "The Macon Meteor" from Georgia sports information director Dan Magill.)

It didn't take the upperclassmen long to take notice. The following Tuesday, after football practice, Henderson was in his front yard on

Columbus Street when a strange car stopped in front of the house.

"Jim Nolan was driving," said Billy. "He wanted to know if I could go with them to a friend's house for a (Phi Omega Beta) fraternity meeting. So I got in the car and went with them."

Even though he was small in stature, Henderson never let the attention cause his head to swell so much it wouldn't fit through the locker room door.

"There was never a problem with overconfidence for any of us," he said. "It was drilled in me to work hard every day. The coaches had a way of creating competition and putting the team first."

But even the underclassmen recognized his potential.

"Billy was one of the chosen, and he lettered at age 14," said Wanninger. "That was a feat that was almost unheard of at Lanier."

For Henderson, carrying the football was as natural as breathing and eating.

"He had moves we had only seen on highlight films at the movies," said Wanninger. "He could spin like a top, stiff arm and, if all else failed, simply out-run them or run over them."

It helped that he was running behind fullback Tom Corn who, at 6-foot-2, 200 pounds, was huge by the standards of the day.

He did get knocked around, though. Wanninger remembers the trainer had to use a roll of tape on Henderson for almost every game. After a road game against Savannah High his freshman season, Henderson suffered a concussion. That night at the hotel, while he was getting dressed, he kept looking around for a missing sock. It wasn't until later that Wanninger looked down at Billy's feet and solved the mystery. He had put two socks on the same foot.

He suffered a freak accident during baseball season his ninth grade year. He was running up the steps at neighborhood friend Arthur Schmidt's house, and his right arm went through the glass door. The cut required stitches. He missed the rest of the season, but still lettered.

His sophomore year, Henderson became a starter in Lanier's backfield and also played safety. He seldom came off the field.

The Poets went 6-4 that year and, led by the sophomore youth movement, began to stockpile the experience that would make them one of the premiere teams in state high school football over the next two years.

The youngsters took their lumps, too. Henderson recalls the 1943 season opener against Columbus. The Poets not only got beat, but battered and bruised. And their strategy didn't work, either.

On Friday morning, the Lanier players boarded the bus for the trip to

Columbus. In an effort to gain a psychological edge, Davis thought he had a good plan against the highly-favored Columbus team.

"Mercer had discontinued their program after the 1942 season, and had offered Coach Davis some of their old uniforms," said Lanier quarterback Carl "Bulldog" Hudson. "The uniforms, although they were old and ragged, were accepted. So we dressed out for the Columbus game in yellow pants and white jerseys. Coach Davis explained in our pre-game meeting that the Columbus players would see the ragged uniforms and would feel they wouldn't have to exert the maximum effort to defeat a team with such equipment."

It didn't work. Columbus won 36-6.

"As the game progressed, it was obvious tricks were not going to affect the outcome," said Hudson.

Henderson scored his team's only touchdown and led the Poets in tackles from his safety position.

"Both Bulldog (Hudson) and I were crying," Henderson said. "We were really whipped. I remember his lower lip sticking out. We were so beat up we climbed up in the luggage rack to sleep on the bus trip home."

Those bus rides home weren't always easy for another reason. There were times when the bus would stop at a store along the way to let the players get out and buy snacks.

But living in a household where there never was a lot of money, Henderson would not even get off the bus.

"I would always pretend to be asleep," he said.

By his junior year, Henderson had emerged as the brightest star in a galaxy of Poet stars. But the biggest transformation of his life took place off the field the summer before his junior season.

Pop Pearson had asked him to serve as a counselor at Athens Y Camp in Tallulah Falls. Coach Davis paid his way for the six-week camp, going around to all the businesses in Macon to ask for contributions.

He may not have been bigger physically when he reported for practice in the fall, but he grew as a person after his summer experience.

"Next to my mother, the biggest spiritual influence on my life was Athens Y Camp," he said. "My convictions matured. You didn't go around talking about it. You saw it. The motto was: 'Where God and Good Times are Friends.'"

As a junior, Henderson was well on his way toward establishing himself as the state's top player for the next two seasons.

He grabbed the headlines almost every week. But it was one of his most forgettable games that is etched in his memory.

In a game against Columbus, the junior back fumbled three times.

"The next week, I had to carry the football with me to class and everywhere else I went. I had to eat with it. I had to sleep with it. I had to carry it with me on the bus to Savannah," he said.

On the first play of the game against Savannah, Henderson broke for a 40-yard gain.

Then he fumbled the ball.

In that same season, the young man who had experienced glory on the football field also stared deep into the eyes of tragedy. In a game against Benedictine at Porter Stadium, teammate Lloyd Mote, a senior who had been called up from the junior varsity, broke his neck making a tackle in the fourth quarter. Mote lay crumpled on the ground. As the stadium grew silent, and his teammates gathered around, the coaches and team doctors had concerned looks on their faces.

X-rays later determined Mote had broken his fifth cervical vertebra. He died on Sunday morning, two days after the Friday night game. Services were held at the City Auditorium, and he was laid to rest in Evergreen Cemetery off Houston Avenue. Several Lanier players served as pallbearers.

"Benedictine had a big fullback who broke through into the secondary, and Lloyd came up and tried to tackle him with his head down," said Roger "Red" Wilson. "The guy ran right over him, and his knees caught him in a bad position. It severed his spinal cord. We didn't have any ambulances at the games back in those days. He hung on until Sunday, and then he died.

"His death had a tremendous impact on the team," said Wilson. "At that age, you never think you're going to die. You never think your friends are going to die."

Mote was a year older than Billy, but he knew him. He lived around the corner on Oglethorpe Street. He was one of 12 children. He had a paper route and worked at a local grocery store to help support his family. His mother was a widow.

The Monday after the tragic game, several players did not show up for practice. Their parents kept them home. Mote's death caused fear to rivet through the team.

"Lloyd Mote's mother got on the phone or went to see some of the other parents personally," Henderson recalled. "She reminded those families that Lloyd was happiest when he was on the football field."

The biggest game of the season came against archrival Boys High in front of 17,000 fans at Ponce de Leon Park in Atlanta. Both teams were undefeated. Since there was no Georgia High School Association or state playoff system, it was ultimately for the state championship.

Boys High Coach Shorty Doyal had the Lanier players intimidated before the game ever started. He kept his team off the field during pre-game warm-ups, and Lanier players were looking over their shoulders every few minutes for their opponents' whereabouts. Then, shortly before kickoff, the band began playing the Boys High fight song. One by one, the Boys High players ran onto the field, 5 yards apart.

"It took them forever to get out there," Henderson said. "They dressed out as many as they could."

Boys High used a trick play on its first possession, gaining 45 yards on a pass play, then scoring three plays later. It marked the first time the Poets had trailed in a game all season.

Although Henderson rushed for 143 yards on 25 carries, Lanier lost the game, 14-6, despite three goal-line stands. Henderson scored his team's only touchdown, but he also fumbled on the 1-yard line as Lanier was marching in for a score.

By the end of his junior year of high school, Henderson's reputation as a football player was superseded only by his enormous talent as a baseball player.

A catcher, he led his high school team in extra base hits and a .411 batting average, and Lanier won the Georgia Interscholastic Athletic Association (GIAA) baseball championship for the second straight year.

Henderson was selected to represent Georgia in the All-American Boys Baseball Game at the Polo Grounds in New York in August 1945. At first, he declined the invitation to participate. His coaches later convinced him to accept. The team was drafted as part of a promotion by Esquire magazine. It was a huge honor, the most prestigious all-star game in the country for prep baseball players.

"The coaches told me it was the opportunity of a lifetime," he said. "I had hardly been out of Macon."

One of the South's most famous sports writers, O.B. Keeler, of "The Atlanta Journal," accompanied Henderson as a chaperone on the trip and wrote about the chronicles of the young man from Macon. (Keeler was author of the famous biography of golfer Bobby Jones called "Down the Fairway.")

Henderson and Keeler made the trip to New York on the train, just weeks after a U.S. Army Air Corps B-25 bomber crashed into the 79th floor of the Empire State Building, killing 14 people.

Traveling was a new world for Henderson. Except for road trips to different cities and towns in Georgia as a high school athlete, the only other place he had ever been was Dublin, where he was born.

He stayed at the New Yorker Hotel in Manhattan. He visited Times Square, Radio City Music Hall and the Empire State Building. He rode the subways and took a ferry up the Hudson River.

The star attractions of the all-star game were the coaches. Babe Ruth was the manager of Henderson's East squad. Ty Cobb was the manager of the West.

"I was 17 years old and all I ever heard about Ty Cobb was that he was a tyrant," Henderson said. "He was aggressive and played dirty. That was always the image I had of him. And Babe Ruth was supposed to be an All-American role model."

At the banquet before the big game, Henderson had a chance to meet Cobb and found out quite the opposite was true.

"I found myself sitting next to this distinguished gentleman in a pinstripe suit," Henderson said. "I chatted with this impressive and refined man throughout the dinner. I later asked a teammate who the man was and he told me. It was Ty Cobb. I had never met a more poised, articulate and considerate person. He impressed me as a genuine and sensitive man."

His image of Ruth would also change.

During the practices before the game on Aug. 28, 1945, Mel Ott, the New York Giants home run king, was the hitting instructor. Henderson also got to catch Giant pitcher (and Hall of Famer) Carl Hubbell, who threw him his famous screwball in batting practice.

"It was like a dream," said Henderson. "I was afraid to pinch myself to find out whether I was awake or not."

The East team would prevail, 5-4, in front of a crowd of 25,000. Branch Rickey, a scout for the Detroit Tigers, was in the stands.

But the story of the game for Henderson happended in the sixth inning. An unfortunate incident took place that would haunt him forever, change his perception of an American sports icon and influence the way he would treat his own players when he would become a high school and college coach.

In the sixth inning, the West team had runners on first and second bases with two outs and a full count on the batter. Henderson was behind the plate, and the East pitcher was left-hander Curt Simmons, who later went on to a 20-year career in the major leagues, most of it spent with the Philadelphia Phillies and St. Louis Cardinals.

The runners were breaking on the 3-2 pitch, but Henderson failed to hear the umpire shout "Ball Four!" He came out of his crouch and tried to throw out the runner streaking toward third base. But the throw sailed over the third baseman's head into the left-field corner. Three runs scored.

"I could have dug a hole at home plate," Henderson said. "Nothing was said in the dugout."

However, when he went out to warm up Simmons at the start of the seventh inning, you could have heard Ruth all the way back in Macon.

"Get me another ....G. D. (expletive) catcher," Ruth yelled.

Stunned, Henderson started taking off his shin guards and chest protector.

"I thought it was the end of the world," he said. "My tears were dropping in the dirt."

But, in its own way, it provided Billy Henderson with a valuable lesson that would later serve him well as a coach of young men. He would threaten his own coaches if they broke this unwritten rule: Never publicly criticize a young athlete for a physical error.

Following the game, a Detroit Tiger scout approached him and wanted to sign him as a catcher. They offered him a $10,000 bonus. He called his mother to get her permission to sign.

"She wouldn't let me," he said. "I figured she would jump on it, but she told me she wanted me to go to school. After she said no, I had so much faith in her that it never crossed my mind again."

Henderson, second from right, watches Babe Ruth give sliding
instructions during practice for the 1945 All-American Boys Baseball
Game at the Polo Grounds in New York. (Photo by Cosmo-Sileo.)

Henderson in his baseball uniform in the Lanier High gym in 1945.
(Photo courtesy of Henderson family.)

'THAT'S MY SON!'

The postman knew the way to Billy Henderson's doorstep at 254 Matheson Drive in 1945. It seemed as if his mailbag was always full of letters from faraway places, bearing postmarks from the cities and towns of colleges trying to convince him to join their team on autumn Saturdays.

Jewell Henderson kept a brown scrapbook with all the letters from colleges that wanted Billy to play football and baseball. On the cover of the scrapbook was an emblem of a pirate with a treasure chest.

The letters came from places she had never been. They were places she would never go. She tried to imagine each campus.

Florida. Alabama. North Carolina. Kentucky. Virginia Military Institute. Tennessee. Wofford. Fresno State. Army. Navy. And, of course, Georgia.

On two occasions, he was invited to attend the Army-Navy game in Philadelphia, but he declined. He never allowed himself to get too caught up in the recruiting process.

He took plenty of phone calls at home from college coaches and recruiters. He was always polite, but also non-committal. Playing his final season at Lanier was his first priority.

Besides, he already had an idea where he was going.

He attended a Georgia game his senior year. There was plenty of fanfare before the game. It was star halfback Charley Trippi's first game back, returning from a three-year stint in the Air Force. He played in the final six games of the season for the Bulldogs in 1945.

Although LSU won the game convincingly, 32-0, Henderson was still fixed on UGA.

"I really didn't have an open mind, because I never thought of going anywhere else but Athens," he said.

His senior season, he went on an official recruiting visit to Georgia Tech in Atlanta for the Georgia-Georgia Tech game at Grant Field.

"The one thing I remember most was Charley Trippi never came off the field," he said. "I was on the sidelines, and I remember on one run he was running toward the Tech bench. But, instead of going out of bounds, he planted his foot and – boom! He broke a tackle and gained an extra 5 yards. Later, as a coach, I used that as a drill."

On the field, Henderson solidified his position as the state's top prep football player.

However, there were some changes in his final season wearing a Poets' uniform. While the country was in the throes of World War II, head coach Stooge Davis was drafted into the Army. (After the war, he was hired as head coach at West Rome High School.)

Cotton Harrison took over as Lanier's head football coach. The Poets didn't miss a beat after the coaching change. Along with Atlanta powerhouses Boys High and Tech High, Lanier was among the elite teams in state high school football.

Henderson scored a GIAA state-record 150 points, giving him 318 for his career, which was also a state record at the time. His single-season scoring mark broke the record of the late Clint Castleberry, who had 114 for Boys High in 1941. Castleberry went on to become an all-SEC halfback for Georgia Tech in 1942 but was drafted into World War II as a B-25 pilot and was killed in action.

Henderson was named a prep All-American for the second straight year. He also made All-Southern, All-GIAA and was rated as the top player in Georgia by "The Atlanta Journal."

"He was able to take advantage of his physical ability and great coaching every step of the way," said Wilson.

Unfortunately, the Poets again fell shy of winning the mythical state championship, falling 26-19 to Tech High at Ponce de Leon Park.

Lanier also lost by an identical 14-6 score to Boys High for the second straight year on a frozen field at Porter Stadium in Macon. The lead on the story in "The Macon Telegraph" the next day said: "The night was cold. The crowd was cold. Henderson was stopped cold."

He was held to 71 yards rushing, his lowest total of the season. Lanier suffered four fumbles, as the Poets lost at home for the first time in two years. Boys High, meanwhile, won its 12th GIAA crown.

But some of the most significant events of his life continued to take place off the field.

It was the Fall of Fosky.

"She rang my bell," he said.

Her name was Frances "Fosky" West. She was born in Atlanta but grew up in Macon. She was the fourth of five children.

Her father, Fred Gardner West, died of pneumonia when she was 2 years old. He named her "Fosky" after a nurse he met in France during World War I.

Her brothers, Ebo and Bob, were colonels in the ROTC program at Lanier.

Fosky was a year older than Billy. She attended Miller High School for Girls and was a cheerleader for Lanier. She worked at the J.W. Griffith Insurance Company, which was located downtown at the Grant Building.

They had a mutual friend, Jeanette Stephenson. She and Fosky were very close.

"He was the town catch, the most handsome thing I ever saw," said Fosky. "Coal black hair. Sparkly eyes. We hit it off real good from the start, and we never broke up."

It was Jesse Duckworth, Jeanette's boyfriend and one of Billy's best friends, who introduced him to Fosky. (He later would be Billy's best man in his wedding.)

Their first date was a hayride at the L Club at Lakeside Park on Oct. 6, 1945. He called her on the phone to ask her out. Jesse had the car that night, so he picked up Billy, too, so they could double date.

Fosky was able to do what many would-be tacklers on the football field were unable to do.

She swept him off his feet.

His strong feelings for her were rivaled only by her attraction to him. She was more interested in the handsome young man who was polite and modest. She was less interested in the star football player who thrilled the football crowds on Friday night with his athletic prowess.

"It was his smile," she said. "It didn't matter to me that he was a football player."

She attended every game. And they began to see each other every available minute of the day.

"I would get on the bus and go see her," Henderson said. "I would ride to town from Bellevue, then get on the Vineville transfer and ride to her house on Vista Circle. Sometimes, if I didn't take the bus, I would walk or run over there."

Often, they would go to movies at one of the downtown theaters – the Grand, the Bibb Theater or the Rialto. On Sundays, they would meet on Cherry Street across from Roy G. Williams Drug Store and walk to church at First Baptist at the top of Poplar Street.

"I would bring her a red carnation every Sunday," he said. "I would buy them for a nickel."

To this day, on their wedding anniversary every Jan. 23, he gives her a dozen red carnations.

"I didn't know I could make a decision in my life whenever I was around Louie Wanninger," he said. "Then Fosky took over. She had my life planned for me."

Of course, Billy never could have dreamed about the cold night in

December, just three days before Christmas, when he committed to play college football for Coach Wally Butts and the Georgia Bulldogs.

Not long after his announcement, he was at the Grand Theater with Fosky. One of the ushers came and told him a college recruiter from South Carolina was there. He was going to give Fosky a scholarship, too, if Henderson would sign.

But Henderson stood solid in his commitment to Georgia. He wasn't the only Lanier player to sign with the Bulldogs. Duckworth also received a scholarship to play in Athens. Hudson signed with Georgia Tech, and Wilson, an all-GIAA end, went to South Carolina.

Yes, it did all seem like a dream.

"It was something I had dreamed about all the way from sandlot to high school," Henderson said. "I had no idea when I started at Lanier High School that any of this would ever happen. When I was 13, I used to go and see the Lanier players in their orange and green uniforms. It was beyond my expectations."

Jewell Henderson never got to see her son play high school football. She was always working. But she reveled in his accomplishments. She kept those scrapbooks of photographs, newspaper clippings and scholarship letters.

And when "The Macon Telegraph" reported Henderson was going to sign with Georgia, she carried a copy of the paper with her on the city bus as she rode to work.

"Billy Henderson," she said, proudly pointing to the newspaper headlines, "That's my son!"

Henderson was a two-time high school All-American in both football and baseball. (Photo courtesy of "The Macon Telegraph.")

Billy and Fosky walk down the steps of Vineville Baptist Church on their wedding day on Jan. 23, 1947. (Photo courtesy of Henderson family.)

MATTERS OF THE HEART

Henderson arrived in Athens for fall football practice in 1946 as one of the most decorated recruits in Georgia's freshman class. In high school, he was clearly the star. In college, he would look around at his teammates and realize every one of them had been stars, too.

They came from football fields in places like Valdosta and Augusta. They had scored touchdowns and made game-saving tackles in the glow of Friday night lights. The headlines in their hometown papers were usually reserved for them, too.

Henderson and Duckworth caught the Greyhound bus from Macon. When they got to Athens, they walked from the bus station on West Broad Street to the athletic dormitory at Milledge Hall.

The first person they saw when they got there was Weyman Sellers, an upperclassman. He was on the floor doing pushups. Another Georgia player, Joe Chesna, was counting. 76 ... 77 ... 78 ... 79 ...

Henderson turned to his high school teammate.

"Jesse," he said, "I think we're in the wrong place."

By 1946, Wally Butts was well on his way to becoming one of Georgia's greatest coaches. Butts, who coached the Bulldogs from 1939-60, won four Southeastern Conference championships, took the Dogs to eight bowl games and was inducted into the College Football Hall of Fame.

He was considered by many to be one of college football's most innovative coaches, particularly in the passing game. Quarterback Fran Tarkenton, who would star for Butts in the late 1950s, once said Butts "knew more football than any other man I ever met."

Butts had been a star at Mercer, playing on the same field, Porter Stadium, where Henderson had been a standout at Lanier. He graduated from Mercer in May 1928, one month before Henderson was born.

Maybe he saw something of himself in Henderson. He, too, was a multi-sport star. He also was small, only 5-foot-5, 155 pounds. But he was a fierce competitor. He even looked like a bulldog.

On the first day of practice, Butts let Henderson know, in no uncertain terms, that those 14 varsity letters he earned in high school meant nothing at the next level.

"I did something wrong during practice. He looked me in the eye and chewed me out," Henderson said. "My shoelace was untied. I reached down to tie it. The next thing I knew, I was on my back. He had flattened me out. That got everybody's attention. I later learned he always picked some player every year and made them an example."

Off the field, Butts might have been considered meek and mild, at least by football standards. But, on the field, the players used to say the grass died under his feet.

His expectations were as high as any coach who ever coached the game. Henderson remembered another legendary preseason practice at the beginning of his freshman year. The team went on the field at 3 p.m. that afternoon. Practice was supposed to be finished by 5 p.m. Only Butts wasn't satisfied with the effort from his team, so he kept them longer.

"It was in the summer and very hot," Henderson recalled. "When 7 o'clock rolled around, I started to get worried. We practiced at Sanford Stadium, back when it had the old lights. When it got dark, Coach Butts told someone to turn on the lights. He wasn't satisfied. He used different words than that, but we got the idea. I think it was 11 o'clock when practice ended. We had people falling by the wayside. I have never hurt or been so tired in all my life. That was Coach Butts' way of showing everyone that to play, you paid a price."

Butts' choice of language was a major adjustment for Henderson. In high school, about the strongest word to come out of Stooge Davis' mouth was "golly doodle."

"Coach Butts questioned my birthright every day," he said. "He cursed like a sailor. Every other word out of his mouth was some kind of profanity. He sounded like a machine gun."

If Butts wasn't intimidating enough, Henderson found himself a boy among men. He was 18 years old. Trippi, who had been in the service, was 26.

"Guys like Trippi and Joe Geri had been on the battlefield," Henderson said. "How was college football going to faze them? They had been shot at.

"Me? All of it scared me to death. I was in awe."

It didn't help that his heart was 85 miles and five counties to the south in Macon. There were times when he was terribly homesick. He was lovesick almost around the clock.

"I set a record traveling that road between Macon and Athens," he said.

During the season, football players were not permitted to leave campus to return home. Henderson ignored all the rules. He didn't have a car, so he had to find ways to get home and back. Most of the time, he hitchhiked. One time, he caught a ride with three students from

Americus. They had a wreck on the way down between Monticello and Macon. The car flipped over three times. Fortunately, no one was hurt.

The classroom brought its own set of challenges. It wasn't that high school had not prepared him for the rigors of college. He had benefited from wonderful teachers at Lanier.

It's just that he poured his heart and soul into sports. Everything else was secondary.

"The first day we had registration, I looked up and saw a line for industrial arts and education," Henderson said. "I had no idea what that was. I'm challenged when it comes to anything to do with shop. I have to have people fix my own mailbox. But I signed up for it anyway."

He made an "A" in English 101, which was theme writing. But he struggled in most of his other classes. Georgia's freshman coach, Howell Hollis, pulled him aside one day.

"What do you want to do when you graduate?" he asked Henderson.

"I want to play major league baseball or coach," Henderson said.

"Well, at the rate you're going, you may play baseball but you won't coach," Hollis said.

It was a wake-up call for Henderson. "A turning point," he said. "I got on the stick and learned to study."

He realized he would have to hit the books just as hard as he hit defenders on the football field.

College professors weren't always willing to give athletes a free pass when it came to their academic work.

Quinton Lumpkin, a former Georgia football standout in the 1930s, was an assistant on the Dogs' coaching staff. He was assigned to accompany Henderson to meet with a geography professor. Henderson was making a 69 in the class. He needed to pull up his grade by one point to pass.

"Can't you let him take the test again?" Lumpkin pleaded. "He's so close."

The professor leaned across the desk.

"Look," he said. "When you're playing football and you gain 9 yards, they don't give you a first down."

Henderson failed the course but went to summer school and passed to stay academically eligible for his sophomore season.

He decided to declare a double major in history and education. A big influence was Dr. Horace Montgomery in the History Department.

"His teaching method was so interesting," Henderson said. "His technique was profound. He gave three pop quizzes per week. I learned to study and always be prepared."

While he learned to study, he also learned how to be an understudy. He knew Trippi, a senior, would get most of the carries and offensive workload and also get most of the snaps at safety. Still, he got significant playing time for a freshman.

"I had to take his licks in practices during the week." Henderson said. "Coach Butts didn't want him to get hit, so they would hit me. But I was privileged to be around the most complete football player of all time. He could do it all. Run. Pass. Kick. And play safety."

As a senior, Trippi led the SEC in scoring with 84 points and had 1,366 yards of total offense (744 rushing and 622 passing). He was runner-up to Army halfback Glenn Davis for the Heisman Trophy and won the Maxwell Award, given to the most valuable player in the country each year.

In 1942, led by Heisman Trophy winner Frank Sinkwich, the Bulldogs had finished 11-1, beaten UCLA in the Rose Bowl and were considered by many to be the mythical national champs.

Four years later, with an undefeated team, it was hard to dispute Georgia's standing at the top of the college football world once again. The Dogs would finish as the nation's only unbeaten and untied team. However, there were no wire service polls at the end of the season, so the declaration of a national champion was always up for debate.

Georgia carried its perfect record into its Sugar Bowl showdown against North Carolina. After coming from behind in the second half to beat the Tar Heels, 20-10, the Georgia players had reason to celebrate their 11-0 season.

Back at the hotel, his teammates put on their coats and ties and headed off to Bourbon Street in New Orleans.

Henderson had other plans.

He called Fosky.

"When I left for college, our intention was to wait four years and get married," he said.

He waited four months.

"Let's get married," he said on the phone.

He told assistant coach J.B. "Ears" Whitworth of his intentions. (Whitworth was later head coach at Alabama from 1955-57, one year prior to Paul "Bear" Bryant.) He left the hotel, most of his teammates still out partying in the French Quarter, and caught the train to Macon.

They were married on Jan. 23, 1947, at Vineville Baptist Church in Macon. They left from the Terminal Station in Macon and rode the train to Jacksonville, Fla., for their honeymoon in St. Augustine.

Getting down there was no problem. Getting back was an entirely different situation.

"I didn't realize I had bought one-way tickets," Henderson said. "I didn't have any money in my pocket, so I became a promoter. I found out who was in charge. It was a man named S.C. Woodard. He was a football fan and knew I was a player for Georgia. I told him we had to get back to Macon, and he said under one condition: I would give him my Georgia-Florida football tickets for the next three years. And that's what I did. He got all four tickets I was allotted every year."

It was not against team rules for players to be married. In fact, several of the upperclassmen, including Trippi, Rabbit Smith, Johnny Rauch and Porter Payne all had wives.

With Henderson, though, it was different. He had not cleared his plans with Butts following the Sugar Bowl victory.

"He never said anything verbally," said Henderson. "But I later learned that I should have gotten permission from him. When you played football for Wally Butts, he was in charge of your life."

Henderson played halfback for the Georgia Bulldogs. (Photo courtesy of University of Georgia Athletic Department.)

BROKEN FIELD RUN

The Macon Meteor had his moments.

Some days were diamonds. Some days were coal.

Henderson figured he would have to wait his turn to make an impact on the football field. But, from the beginning, he made his mark on the baseball diamond.

He hit .350 his freshman season and beat team captain Howard Johnson out of his job. Butts went to baseball Coach J.V. Sikes and ordered him to get Henderson out from behind the plate. He did not want Henderson playing catcher. He was afraid the strain on his knees would affect his speed on the football field.

Also, in the summers of 1948 and '49, he played for Wrightsville in the old Ogeechee League. The mayor of Wrightsville was good friends with Butts, who encouraged Henderson to play for the team.

Henderson enjoyed spending his summers riding buses on back roads in the bush leagues. He earned some money, and the running kept him in shape for football season.

Going into the 1947 season, Edwin Pope, who went on to become one of America's best-known sports writers, described Georgia's backfield situation like this:

"The left halfback position is as wide open as the 1948 Presidential election, and there are just as many candidates."

Henderson was the starter for most of the year, and also ranked among the nation's leaders in kickoff returns with a 26.5-yard average His 12 returns for 319 yards established a school record.

The team finished 7-4-1 and tied Maryland in the Gator Bowl. In the game, Henderson caught a 58-yard pass from quarterback Rauch which was, at the time, a Gator Bowl record.

The season also brought its share of personal joy. Billy and Fosky were living in a one-room apartment on Buena Vista Avenue in Athens. In December, Fosky found out she was pregnant.

Billy Henderson was going to become a dad.

He continued to excel at baseball, hitting a career-high .410 for the Dogs his sophomore season. (He is one of only nine players in Georgia history to hit better than .400 in a season.)

He also played his first season in Wrightsville. The team made the playoffs, and the extended season cut into the beginning of football.

Butts encouraged his football players to continue with Wrightsville in the playoffs, even if it meant missing football practice.

On Aug. 15, 1948, Henderson was getting ready to play in a game in Wrightsville when he got word Fosky was in labor. He hurried to Athens, where Fosky gave birth to a son. They named him William Bradford Henderson Jr.

The weight of his busy life began to bear down on Billy's shoulders. The joy of becoming a father for the first time was tempered with the demands of finishing baseball season and starting football season.

The transition was physically exhausting. Three straight days, Henderson passed out from heat exhaustion. He had been working out at night and was not prepared for the heat of the sun. Several of his Georgia teammates, who also played in the Ogeechee League, quit the football team because of the demands of playing two sports.

Baseball season had taken its toll on his body. Then came the rigors of two-a-days in football. The baby was crying constantly. He couldn't rest. He was burning the candle at both ends.

He would do his best to help Fosky with the baby, often getting up with Brad for those late-night feedings. There were times when the only way he thought he could pacify Brad was by sticking his big toe in Brad's mouth.

He looked at the depth chart. He had fallen to No. 6 at the halfback position.

"My first reaction was to tell myself I would show them," he said. "I knew I had overextended myself. My next reaction was to pout. I got to where I wasn't speaking to the coaches. Some of my teammates said I pouted all the way to the Orange Bowl."

He returned kicks and played sparingly. The Bulldogs finished the regular season 9-1, winning the SEC championship before falling to Texas in the Orange Bowl.

Meanwhile, one of Brad's playmates was Billy Payne, the son of Henderson's UGA teammate Porter Payne. (Billy Payne would later go on to play football at Georgia for Vince Dooley and gained international fame as the man who brought the 1996 Summer Olympics to Atlanta.)

His junior year in baseball, he hit .350, earning all-SEC honors as a right-fielder and leading the conference in stolen bases.

He also continued to play for Wrightsville in the Ogeechee League, hitting .345 in 1948 and .380 in 1949. He was earning a decent enough salary for a semipro league.

In those days, having a local baseball team was important to small towns throughout rural Georgia. And the rivalries between towns were often fierce, much the same way it was on Friday nights during high school football season.

Henderson remembers one such road game against Glenville in 1948. He had reached third base but, on a squeeze play, broke too quickly for the plate. The pitcher wheeled and threw to the third baseman who, in turn, threw to the catcher.

"The catcher was blocking the plate with a big smile on his face," Henderson said. "So I ran him over and scored. The ball went one way and the mitt went the other way. After I went back to the dugout, the umpire ruled I had interfered with the catcher and called me out. Our pitcher ran out of the dugout onto the field and decked the umpire.

"Both benches emptied. I didn't fight. I ran. But I did have a bat thrown at me. Fans from both sides jumped the fence in center field. The local cops were just laughing. I think they were enjoying it."

Henderson was not only concerned for his own safety, but for that of his young brother-in-law, Bob Hearn, who had come to watch Henderson play.

"My first reaction was: What am I going to tell his mother?" said Henderson. "He was smart, though. He hid under the bench in the dugout."

By his senior year in football, his role had diminished to only a part-time contributor. A knee injury hampered him both his junior and senior seasons.

While he continued to clutch those dreams of playing major league baseball, he knew his days as a football player were numbered.

It was not an easy realization.

"Looking back, I realize I wasn't in Coach Butts' plans, or he never would have allowed me to go to Wrightsville my junior year," Henderson said. "It was difficult not to be playing, and I never really knew where I stood with him. Without question, that experience made me a better coach later on. I would communicate with my players. I knew how it felt to sit on a bench."

Henderson certainly wasn't the only big-name high school football recruit who didn't quite measure up in college. Even today, almost six decades later, the memories of his college football days are numb with regret.

"A dark cloud has always been over my head that I never lived up to those expectations of me," he said. "I had realized my potential in high school. College was a different matter. Of course, I only weighed 160 pounds. That might have had something to do with it."

Henderson found solace on the baseball field. He led the Dogs in hitting three straight years. His senior year, he was team captain. He hit .386 and stole a conference-leading 29 bases in 29 games, a school record that stood for 30 years.

"It was always fun for me to run the bases," Henderson said. "Coach Jim Whatley always gave me the green light."

He was the captain of Jim Whatley's first team (Whatley coached Georgia for 24 years.) Henderson was a three-time All-SEC selection and hit .375 for his college career, the sixth-highest career average in school history.

His 91 career stolen bases are still a Georgia record.

After college, he signed a baseball contract with the Macon Peaches, in the Chicago Cubs farm system. William Fickling Sr., a local real estate developer and civic leader, owned the team.

So the little boy who had once chased down foul balls at Luther Williams Field just so he could get a free pass into the stadium, was going to play in his hometown.

Henderson got a $2,500 signing bonus. He and Fosky bought a new car, a Ford, from Heyward Allen Motors in Athens. He made his professional debut on June 2, 1950, his 22nd birthday. There was a lot of local excitement surrounding the game, and a huge crowd turned out at Luther Williams Field.

In the other dugout, the players for Jacksonville were riding him the entire game.

"They kept calling me 'rookie' and 'hometown boy,'" said Henderson. "They were dogging me big-time. Even though I was a left-handed hitter, I wasn't getting around on the pitches. In my first at-bat, I fouled off nine straight pitches into their third base dugout."

He finished the game going 1-for-4. After three weeks, he was already wearing another uniform. While hitting .333, he left to finish the season with the Class D Fitzgerald Pioneers. There, he hit .370 and stole 63 bases.

To earn money for his family in the offseason, he was hired as manager of Adams-Feagin Hardware Store in Macon.

In 1951, he was among the players invited to spring training with the Cubs in Palatka, Fla. It was a big thrill, a lifelong dream. But the rites of spring also carried a hollow ring.

Henderson believed his best shot at making a major league roster was at second base because of his quickness. He found himself as a reserve outfielder when he returned to Macon to start the season, where he hit over .300.

By June, he had been assigned to Greenville, S.C. The day he arrived, he went 5-for-7 and stole two bases in a double-header.

But was he happy? He asked himself that question the next morning as he drank coffee at the hotel where he was staying in Greenville.

He wasn't sure how many more bus rides he had in him.

"My family was back in Macon," he said. "I was lonely. We had moved from Athens to Macon to Fitzgerald and back to Macon. Now I was in Greenville. I enjoyed playing baseball, but I was impatient. I was 23 years old, and I thought that was old. I felt like I should already be in the big leagues."

So he gathered all his belongings in a bag and returned to Macon.

"It was a snap decision," he said. "It was right in the middle of the season, and management didn't like it at all."

The Macon club assigned him to Hazlehurst-Baxley of the Class D Georgia State League. He played in a Saturday night double-header, then walked away.

A voice inside him was calling. He had contacted Stooge Davis, his old high school coach. Davis had become the head coach in Jefferson, a small town about 20 miles north of Athens.

He had an opening on his staff for an assistant coach.

Billy Henderson, the player, was about to become Billy Henderson, the coach.

Henderson, top left, with Jefferson High School baseball team in 1952. (Photo courtesy of Henderson family.)

'COACH'

Billy and Fosky Henderson had the kind of furniture that had been moved so many times it would practically hop on the truck when they snapped their fingers. Now, it was time to move again.

Henderson returned to Macon, confident this was the first day of the rest of his life.

Coach Henderson.

He liked the way that sounded.

For the next 45 years, he would hear it millions of times.

While getting ready for the move to Jefferson, Henderson took a temporary job working in the meat department at Mulberry Market. Then he and Fosky packed 3-year-old Brad and all their worldly possessions in a pickup truck with no cover.

"What if it rains?" Fosky asked on the way up.

"Oh, no, it won't rain," said Henderson, the eternal optimist.

It rained all the way from Macon to Jefferson.

Morris Bryan owned Jefferson Mills. He was the most influential man in Jefferson, a man whose arm had been mangled in a mill accident when he was younger. He was heavily involved with the local high school, the recreation department and later was the driving force behind the annual all-classification state track meet in Jefferson. He also taught Sunday School.

Bryan had told Henderson he had made temporary living arrangements for him and his family when they got there. When they arrived, it was night, and they rode down red clay roads to what turned out to be the local Boy Scout hut. It was dark. There was no electricity.

"It was one of the longest nights of my life," Henderson said.

Then, daylight came and they found a home to rent on Nicholson Road. That same day, Henderson met Carol Bufford, who would become a trusted friend.

Bufford also coached at the high school and had been hired by Bryan to be in charge of the recreation department.

It wasn't long before Henderson learned what a fierce competitor Bufford was. In a game of touch football, Bufford came out of nowhere and unloaded on Henderson.

The friendship soon blossomed and prospered. It became a mutual admiration society. Later, Henderson would name his daughter, Carol, after Bufford, and Bufford named his son, Billy, after Henderson.

Later in Henderson's coaching career, Bufford was going with him to start the program at Macon's Willingham High. But Bufford instead took the head job in his hometown of Lincolnton, where he won a Class C state title with a 12-0 record, the school's first unbeaten and untied team. Stricken with cancer, he coached his final year at Lincolnton in a wheelchair.

"As he lay there dying, people would come to cheer him up," Henderson said. "Instead, he was the one who cheered them up."

He died at age 33.

Henderson was greatly influenced by his association with Jefferson Community Day Camp in the summer of 1951. It was run by Jefferson Mills and gave local youngsters a summer camp full of recreational opportunities at Memorial Park.

As the start of football practice approached, Henderson felt a tremendous peace. Some athletes have a hard time adjusting when their playing careers are over. But Henderson had embraced his decision. When God shuts a door, He opens a window.

"I had this deep-rooted faith that there was no question we were going to make it," he said. "Whenever I was on an athletic field, I was confident. I had been equipped by the best."

It helped that Stooge Davis was there to serve as his mentor. The coach who had been a major influence on his life as a high school player was now his boss.

"He was a sound football coach in the areas of blocking, tackling, drills and conditioning," Henderson said. "He was light years ahead of everybody else when it came to weight training. He always believed his players needed to be doing something physical every day – even on Saturdays, Sundays and holidays."

Although his admiration for Davis grew even stronger, it was also tempered by reality. He saw his coach in a different light.

"In my mind, he was always the perfect man," Henderson said. "I named my youngest son, Johnny, after him. I had an idealistic view of him when I was in high school. Later, when I started coaching with him, I realized he wasn't perfect. He was human."

A.W. Ashe was the principal at Jefferson. He demanded a lot out of his teachers. He was a perfectionist who expected every faculty member to keep his or her classroom neat and organized.

Henderson was so nervous about his teaching duties he would prepare his lesson plans weeks ahead of time. He was assigned to teach history, civics, mechanical drawing and be the driver's education instructor. Ashe also asked him to teach algebra.

"I think too much of these kids to do that," he said.

His coaching duties were just as demanding as his teaching load. He was backfield coach for the Dragons that year, as Jefferson went 7-3. He became a student of the game. He observed how Davis handled the players. He was learning from a true master.

He also coached both the boys and girls basketball squads.

And, since he was the driver's ed teacher, naturally he drove the team bus, too.

One winter's night in 1952, Jefferson traveled to Pickens County to play a basketball double-header.

"Here I was, a 23-year-old coach with boys and girls on the bus, and we were driving back late at night," he said. "Back in those days, we would drop off some of the players at his or her house before returning to the school. I had to travel down a lot of rural dirt roads."

One such road ran beside Jefferson Mills.

"It was late at night, and I had to get up the next morning and go work in the spinning department at the mill at 6 a.m.," said Marvin Hall, a junior who was on the bus. "There was a railroad trestle, and the road went to one lane beneath it. I was sitting in the seat right behind Coach Henderson. It looked wide enough and he said: 'Watch this!'"

"He was looking at the width but wasn't thinking about the height. He didn't even hit his brakes. We hit that trestle and came to a complete stop. I remember Coach Henderson had his head down. He asked if everybody was all right."

Said Henderson: "I was the driver's ed teacher. I thought I knew everything. When I hit the trestle, everything got quiet. Fortunately, nobody was hurt. But they were all very quiet."

The bus was wedged in. It took a wrecker to pull it out the next morning. In the meantime, Henderson got the players back to the school and returned home. But his conscience was bothering him. At 4 a.m., he got up, got dressed and went to principal Ashe's house to tell him.

The next Monday, there was a banner up at school: "Coach Henderson, Driver's Ed Teacher, Wrecked the Bus."

He never heard the end of it.

The boys basketball team had a successful season, winning the district. The girls, however, were a different story. The Lady Dragons went 0-19. Henderson did everything he could to keep up the morale. Stella Ashe, the wife of the principal, gave him a lot of help handling the girls since he didn't have an assistant. Henderson often solicited advice from Tom Porter, his old high school coach.

In the spring, Henderson was responsible for starting a baseball program – from scratch.

"I went to Coach Davis and asked him where the uniforms were," Henderson said. "He said there weren't any. There weren't any bats. There weren't any balls. The next day he gave us three balls."

So Henderson knocked on doors. It would be the beginning of a reputation he would develop in coaching. When Billy Henderson needed something, he kept asking for it until he got it.

"People even joked that when folks saw me walking down the sidewalk, they would cross over to the other side," he said, laughing. "They knew I wanted something."

He got equipment from local merchants. The mothers of the players made the uniforms from material provided by Jefferson Mills.

When it came to coaching football, Henderson read as much as he could about the subject. Weeks before the kickoff to the 1952 season, he told Davis he believed he could benefit from attending the coaches clinic held in conjunction with the annual North-South All-Star Game at Grant Field in Atlanta.

Legendary Valdosta Coach Wright Bazemore was coaching the South team.

"One of my goals in life was to one day coach in that game," Henderson said. "Wright Bazemore was also one of my heroes. I used to carry a picture of him around in my wallet."

Because of limited athletic department funds, Henderson was somewhat reluctant about asking Davis for money to attend the clinic. But Davis said he would be more than happy to give him some money to cover expenses.

"The next day, he handed me an envelope," said Henderson. "I raced home and opened it up. There was a check for $1.75."

Henderson attended the clinic anyway and stayed in the Georgia Tech dormitory for 50 cents per night.

"I was walking down Peachtree with some of my buddies and saw Davis coming out of a nice hotel," he said, laughing.

It wasn't just a matter of learning the system. Henderson began to gain experience in all aspects of running a high school football program. Part of it, like first-aid and taping ankles, came through on-the-job training.

The football team finished 7-3 again that fall. Henderson also was assigned to coach the boys basketball team, but the school had hired a young teacher, Patsy Evans, to coach the winless girls squad from the year before. Evans was a native of Wrens and had recently graduated from Georgia Southern.

With all the girls returning, there was hope for marked improvement. Then, early in the 1952-1953 season, Evans was killed in an automobile accident.

"It was the first time I had experienced death like that," Henderson said. "They asked me to coach the girls for the rest of the season. We put it behind us and had a winning season."

After his baseball team recorded its second straight winning season, Henderson began to attract a few offers from other schools. One offer came from Monroe High School, which was looking for a head football coach.

"I was tempted but, looking back, I was wise not to take it," he said.

That's because Weyman Sellers, his former Georgia teammate, was the head coach at Athens High School, which later became Clarke Central.

Sellers was looking for an offensive and defensive backfield coach and head baseball coach.

He offered the job to Henderson, who left behind two happy years in Jefferson to take another step up the coaching ladder.

After all, Athens High was a good situation. It reminded him of another school.

"It was a duplication of Lanier," he said. "They had committed teachers and students. They had an ROTC program. There was a lot of school spirit. It was a great experience to be there."

Of course, it didn't hurt that a talented young ninth-grade quarterback named Fran Tarkenton arrived at the same time.

"Even at a young age, he was the epitome of leadership and confidence," Henderson said. "He was so gifted as an athlete. Everything came easy for him."

Billy, Fosky, Brad and 1-year-old Fran settled into a small apartment complex called Myrna Court, just a long post pattern away from the school. Henderson was assigned to teach five subjects.

His first summer there in 1953, Henderson went over to meet some of the players and participate in a touch football game. Sellers told him to captain one of the teams, and he would give him the first pick.

"I didn't know any of them, so I went on looks," he said. " We got whipped, and I learned a very valuable lesson that day. You can't measure a person's heart."

The school also needed a swimming coach. It was Henderson who raised his hand.

"I don't think he knew which end of the pool to get in," laughed Jimbo Laboon, a member of the swim team.

Said Henderson: "They needed a volunteer. I was a poor swimmer, at best, but that didn't seem to matter."

No, it didn't. Athens won the state championship in swimming that year. To celebrate, the swimmers threw their coach into the pool. That would have been fine, except that he couldn't get out.

That same year, Henderson went in the water for another reason. Although he had been baptized by sprinkling as a youngster in Macon, he was baptized by immersion by the Rev. Howard Giddens, at the First Baptist Church of Athens.

"Dr. Giddens touched my heart that day," said Henderson. "He made me see the necessity of professing Christ publicly and leading a Christ-like life."

The 1954 Athens High team was a state contender, making it all the way to the state quarterfinals against Rockmart. Sellers sent Henderson to scout a game at Jesup, where his former UGA backfield mate, John Donaldson, was the coach. Henderson was so confident Athens had won its game against Rockmart, that he flipped coins with Donaldson after the game to see which team would wear its home jerseys in the semifinal matchup.

Then he heard on the radio returning home that Athens had lost on the last play of the game. After attempting a pass, an Athens player fumbled and it was returned by Rockmart for a touchdown.

Donaldson wasn't the only former Georgia teammate Henderson would shake hands with in the final weeks of the 1954 season. Homer Hobbs, who played with Henderson from 1946-48, had left his coaching position at Navy to become the head coach at Furman. Joining him on the Furman staff was another of Henderson's UGA teammates, Johnny Griffith.

Hobbs asked Henderson to make the jump from high school to college coaching and join them on the Furman staff.

The Athens High players and coaching staff gave their popular assistant coach a farewell party in the school's basement. John Simpson, a member of the team who later would become the director of the Athens Y Camp and YMCA, stood up and gave a speech. He reflected on the contributions Henderson had made in his two years on the staff.

"I had a lump in my throat," Henderson said. "My heart hurt. I remember driving up the highway thinking how in the world they were ever going to make it without me."

The next year, Athens High won the state title.

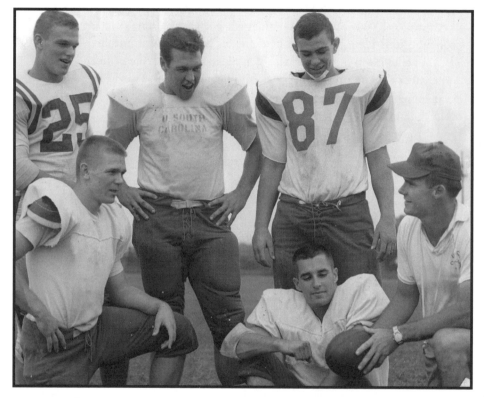

Henderson with South Carolina players in 1957. (Photo courtesy
of South Carolina Athletic Department.)

BIG LEAGUES

The last time Billy Henderson had been to Greenville, S.C., it was literally for a cup of coffee. It was for the double-header he played with Greenville during the 1951 season, where he ultimately made his decision to give up baseball in a coffee shop that Sunday morning.

As he left Athens High for his next calling, he was hopeful he would be there for an extended stay. He was excited about the opportunity to coach at the next level. At the time, he said his goal was to become a head football coach at the college level.

He knew there would be a period of adjustment. But it wasn't like he was embarking on some brave, new world.

"Football is football," he said. "The only difference is the players are bigger and faster."

There was yet another difference. It was called a budget.

He and assistant Johnny Griffith made a request to attend the American Football Coaches Association convention. The next thing they knew, they were holding airline tickets to Los Angeles.

"I had a little more than $1.75 this time," he said, laughing.

The first season, the Paladins went 1-9, their lone win coming against The Citadel. They finished ranked 109th out of the 111 teams in the NCAA Division IA power rankings.

"Johnny (Griffith) and I joked we set football back 100 years," Henderson said. "Army beat us 81-0 that year up at West Point. After the game, we went to their mess hall to eat. As we were eating, their cadets started counting. By the time they got to 15, we realized what they were doing. When they got to 81, they all threw their caps up in the air."

After that disastrous first year, recruiting became a top priority. It was his responsibility to scout the best and the brightest prep players. He would sit in their living rooms with their mamas and daddies and try to convince them to sign a letter of intent to play for Furman.

Because of his tremendous people skills, Henderson proved to be a good recruiter. He remembers one recruiting trip he and Griffith took when they got lost in the hills of east Tennessee.

"We don't know where this road is going," said Griffith, " but we sure are making good time."

During one recruiting trip, they were sharing a motel room. Always an early riser, Henderson got up to eat breakfast while Griffith slept. He was reading the newspaper when he saw a headline on the sports page: "Son of Furman Aide Stricken With Polio."

Henderson's heart stopped. He thought it was Brad. Then he read the story. It was Buzzy Griffith, Johnny's son.

"He drove so fast on those mountain roads to get home I've never been so happy to get to my destination," Henderson said.

The good news was that Buzzy recovered from his bout with polio.

After one year, Griffith returned to Athens as an assistant on Butts' staff. (He later would become Georgia's head coach from 1961-63.)

Henderson's other duty at Furman was to coach the track team. It was at a track meet in Clinton, S.C., he met Warren Giese, the head coach at South Carolina. Giese had left the staff at Maryland under Jim Tatum, one of college football's most innovative minds and a coach who had a profound influence on the philosophies of such coaches as Paul "Bear" Bryant, Woody Hayes and Bud Wilkinson. Giese brought with him many of Tatum's ideas, including the Split T offense.

Giese knew of Henderson's reputation as a recruiter. He was so impressed after meeting him he offered him a job as head freshman coach.

"It was tempting, but it wouldn't have been the right thing to do that close before the (1956) season," Henderson said. "I told him the timing wasn't right. I didn't want to let Furman down."

By the middle of the 1956 season, the decision was being made for him. Henderson arrived at the athletic department one morning, got out of his car and saw Frank Sinkwich walking across the parking lot.

He shook hands with Sinkwich, Georgia's first Heisman Trophy winner in 1942, and asked him what he was doing in Greenville.

"I've come up here to help my buddy Homer," Sinkwich said.

Henderson then asked him what he was coaching.

"Offensive and defensive backs," said Sinkwich.

"Oh, really," Henderson said, stunned. That was his job.

Henderson went straight to his office and had the athletic department secretary type his letter of resignation.

"Hobbs was going to demote me," he said.

He called Giese. Was there still a spot for him in Columbia?

"Can you be here at 7 a.m. in the morning?" Giese asked him.

Henderson drove to Columbia, where he met Giese for breakfast. They talked about the possibilities of Henderson joining the staff at mid-season.

For the next week, Henderson got up every day, put on a coat and tie as if he was going to work, and spent the morning at the Poinsettia Hotel in Greenville.

Within a week of his resignation at Furman, Giese gave him the go-ahead to start his new job as freshman coach and offensive backfield coach with the varsity.

As a coach, Giese had a profound influence on Henderson.

"He had tremendous organizational skills," Henderson said. "Every minute had a precise plan. Every practice had objectives. He stressed fundamentals daily and execution was a top priority."

Giese started one of college football's first organized weight programs in Columbia.

At South Carolina, Henderson was on the same staff with Ernie Lawhorn, who had been a star at Lanier and had gone on to play for the Gamecocks. The defensive coordinator was Marvin Bass, who later became South Carolina's head coach and was on Coach Dan Reeves' staff with the Atlanta Falcons.

Henderson coached the remainder of the '56 season, when South Carolina finished with a 7-3 record, and all of 1957, when the Gamecocks sported a 5-5 record.

After the 1957 season, Giese was offered the head coaching job at the University of Houston. He flew out for an interview. When he returned, he was met at the Columbia airport by the mayor and South Carolina boosters. He was given the keys to a new car and persuaded to stay.

He coached three more years, but the honeymoon ended when he couldn't beat Clemson consistently. (He was 1-4). His five-year career mark at South Carolina was 28-21-1. He later was elected a South Carolina state senator.

A chance to remain in Columbia hardly mattered to Henderson. In December 1957, his brother-in-law, Ebo West, told him about a new high school being built in Macon. At the time, Henderson was on a recruiting trip in Orlando, a memorable trip because it was snowing in central Florida for the first time in years. Henderson called Judge Walter Stevens, who was a member of the Bibb County school board. Stevens encouraged him to contact school superintendent Mark Smith.

Smith asked Henderson to come to Macon for an interview. Henderson told Giese about the opportunity before he left.

"He didn't think I was serious about it," said Henderson. "But I had missed working with high school kids. I drove down to Macon, interviewed and we shook hands. They had not even completed the building at the time."

When he returned to Columbia, he told Giese he was leaving.

"He was shocked," Henderson said. "He really didn't think I would go. He asked if I had signed a contract, and I told him I had verbally accepted. He talked to boosters and they tried to give me some incentive to stay, but I had already committed.

"A high school post in Macon was the only high school job I would consider leaving college coaching for," he said. "I had a desire to work with high school boys again. I knew I was ready. I had worked under some of the very best coaches and picked up the best from each of them."

Billy Henderson was going home.

Henderson conducts one of the first football practices at Willingham in March 1958. (Photo courtesy of "The Macon Telegraph.")

Henderson celebrating Willingham's first win over rival Lanier
in 1960. (Photo courtesy of Henderson family.)

HOME TEAM

Billy Henderson brought more to Macon with him than just a wife, four kids, furniture and clothes. He packed a suitcase full of experience. In 10 years as a high school, college and professional athlete, and seven years as an assistant coach, he had picked brains, blistered hands and drawn the lifeblood of every season.

Now, at age 29, he was a head coach. He would be the man in charge. He was ready.

But even the greatest coach in the world has to have players. So Henderson went knocking on doors. He went to every elementary school in South Macon. He even went to Lanier High, where he knew some students would be attending when the doors of Alfred Ross Willingham High School for Boys opened for the first time in the fall of 1958.

"I encouraged every youngster, no matter how big or small or inexperienced," he said. "As long as they were committed and, went by the rules, nobody would be cut."

In February 1958, he sent a letter to every incoming student at the all-male public school. In the letter, he addressed and clarified three concerns.

1. *"I'm too small." Regardless of size, many boys have developed into great athletes, and any prospective athlete at Willingham will be given equal opportunity.*

2. *"I have no transportation home after practice." It should be understood that any boy who participates at Willingham will be given a ride home by a member of the coaching staff.*

3. *"I'm afraid I won't make the squad." It should be understood that no boy will ever be cut from any athletic team at Willingham for lack of ability. There will always be a place for any person interested in our athletic program.*

He was always true to that word. In 45 years of coaching, he never cut a player.

Everything was new. A new school building. A new faculty and coaching staff. There was the opportunity to pick a mascot, school colors and build a tradition.

The first day of spring practice was May 1, 1958, at Porter Stadium. They started in shorts. Henderson's efforts had paid off. There were 175 young men at the first practice. (Willingham went into its first year without a senior class.)

Selby Buck was the athletic director for Bibb County.

"We don't have uniforms and equipment for that many people," he told Henderson.

"Don't worry, we'll find it," Henderson said.

In a vote of the student body, Rams was picked as the mascot. Blue and white were chosen as the school colors. Henderson's first staff was made up of Johnny Stallings, Dave Hill, Martin Allman, Henry Middlebrooks, Bobby Brown and Billy Beale.

The practice field was across from the school on Williamson Road. It was an old cow pasture, and the players often returned from practice smelling of cow manure.

But none of that seemed to matter. The Rams had yet to play their first game, and Henderson was already leading the league in optimism.

"I believed in those kids," he said. "I thought we would win every game. I knew how hard they had worked. I wanted it to happen then."

So did Eddie Battle, who was Henderson's first quarterback.

"Going into every game, he had us so fired up we thought we could beat the Green Bay Packers," said Battle. "We were so high we never even thought about losing. We thought we were going to win every game."

But, the Rams had to take baby steps.

The first game in school history was against Macon's Dudley Hughes, coached by Godfrey "Goot" Steiner, who later went on to coach at Lanier and Central.

The Rams fought to a 0-0 tie, their first of three ties that opening season. The losses began to pile up, although three defeats were by a touchdown or less. The other ties came against Americus (0-0) and Warner Robins (12-12).

"You talk about optimism – Moultrie was coming to town to play us, and I came out in the paper and said we would whip 'em and it wouldn't be a fluke," Henderson said.

Moultrie won the game, 28-0, and Henderson lost his cool. On one play, he believed the Moultrie players were piling on his ball carrier, Bobby Matthews, out of bounds. When the official did not throw his flag, Henderson reached into his pocket and pulled it out for him.

"I slammed it on the ground and asked him how he could not have called that," Henderson said. "It was a dumb thing for me to do. He should have thrown me out of the game, but he walked off 15 yards against Moultrie. I was just so frustrated."

During times like that, when he did get discouraged, Henderson thought of how his mother used to walk home from work in the rain to save the money it took for a bus fare.

As always, Jewell Henderson was his inspiration.

But even a winless season brought its share of bright spots. And Henderson found them.

"You can say every team you coach becomes one of your favorites," he said. "But this group deserves a special place in my heart. They went into every game thinking they would win it. They stuck it out, and didn't give up."

In one game, the Rams fell behind powerhouse LaGrange 39-0. Although the game was out of reach in the fourth quarter, and running back Matthews had been sent to the hospital with a concussion, the Rams took the ball at their own 20-yard line and went 80 yards over the last eight minutes. They scored with a few seconds left on the clock.

"The referee came up to me after the game and told me if we hadn't scored, he was going to put the ball in the end zone for us," said Henderson.

The lumps of the inaugural season in 1958 gave way to success the following year. In the second game of the season, the Rams trounced Dudley Hughes, 34-6, the first of three straight wins. Willingham also had victories over Perry, Americus and Warner Robins on its way to a 6-4 record.

The final game of the season came against Lanier in the first-ever meeting between the two schools. It would be the beginning of one of the city's great rivalries.

Lanier won the game, 19-0. The Poets were coached by Cotton Harrison, Henderson's football coach his senior year in 1945.

After the game, Willingham principal Fred Johnson found Henderson in the school gymnasium.

"I never realized how hard football coaches work," he told Henderson.

But the work was far from done. Henderson was also athletic director and head baseball coach. And, of course, he spent every possible moment planning and preparing for the next football season. It was also the year he started taking the team to football camp every summer.

It was an idea he borrowed from Stooge Davis, who took his Lanier teams to the Athens YMCA camp facilities. The first year, Henderson took the Rams to Lawrenceville's Camp Perrin, which was run by track legend Perrin Walker.

"The brochures said to bring your fishing poles and cameras," said Henderson. "But, when we got there, it was somewhat ... rustic."

After that, Henderson began the longstanding tradition of taking his teams to Jekyll Island. It was a chance for the players and coaches to live, breathe, eat and sleep football beneath the beautiful live oak trees, draped in Spanish moss.

Sure, it was a chance to "get away" from the routine practices in Macon. There was some "free time," too. Players could enjoy the beach and sunshine.

But it was mostly business. It was a boot camp in preparation for the season. Henderson's players could later claim that when they faced difficult situations in life, they found the strength they needed to pull through because they had survived those camps at Jekyll Island.

Willingham put together another winning program in 1960, going 5-4-1. Of all the highlights, three stood above the others.

One, the Rams shut out Moultrie, 19-0, the team that had blanked them by four touchdowns two seasons earlier.

The second was a chance to play Valdosta and its legendary coach, Wright Bazemore. Although the Wildcats won 19-0 on their way to another of Bazemore's 14 state championships at Valdosta, it was a thrill for Henderson to be on the opposing sideline.

"He was the epitome of high school coaches," Henderson said. "I admired the way he played so many boys. He looked like he dressed out the entire student body. He always played as many people as he could to improve morale and gave his players lots of recognition at the football banquet. He could take an average player and instill in him the desire and ability to play over his head."

In 30 seasons at Valdosta, Bazemore was 268-51-7 and his teams were named national champions three times. In addition to the 14 state championships, he was runner-up four times and won 17 region titles.

The biggest moment for the highlight reel came in the season finale against favored Lanier. Willingham took a 6-0 lead into halftime despite running just six offensive plays in the first two quarters, three of them from the shadow of their own goal post.

Jimmy Hammond blocked a Lanier punt, and defensive lineman Lathrop Holder caught it.

"His teammates had to point him to the goal line," recalled Henderson, laughing.

Halfback Clint Tucker led the Rams downfield on a 68-yard march for what proved to be the winning score in a 13-6 victory. He had a 39-yard run to the Lanier 14, then later scored from the 7.

"How we won that game was a miracle," Henderson said. "It proved to be one of our biggest victories of all time. It created confidence that all the hard work had paid off."

By 1961 and '62, Willingham had established itself as one of the rising programs in Class AAA and long-time Willingham camera man Bobby Jones was there to capture it on film. The Rams went 7-2-1 in 1961, losing only to LaGrange and Valdosta – two of the state's premier programs. The season was capped by a 23-6 triumph over Lanier in front of a crowd of 10,500 at Porter Stadium.

Willingham enjoyed a strong relationship with McEvoy, the girls high school next door. McEvoy provided Willingham with its cheerleaders. The schools held pep rallies and bonfires together.

"The spirit was unbelievable," said Henderson.

The week before the Lanier game, it was a tradition for Lanier students to try to kidnap Willingham's ram mascot. So the Willingham boys slept in the gym to guard the ram. They got into their own mischief during the Lanier week. It was all in the spirit of the rivalry. They would run a "Smear Lanier" banner up the flag pole at Lanier.

In 1962, the Rams won three games by a single point, including a 7-6 win over Lanier, and two more games by a touchdown on their way to a 7-1-2 record. Their only loss was to eventual state champion Valdosta.

"Our game against Lanier had one of the outstanding drives in the history of football," Henderson said. "In the fourth quarter, we went 83 yards on 24 plays. We didn't throw a single pass. Our longest gain was 7 yards. It consumed almost the entire fourth quarter (11 minutes.) The stadium was packed. Pete Gaines, our quarterback, scored on fourth down with less than a minute left. It was unbelievable."

The '62 season was also the year Henderson had to convince one of his top running backs, Bobby Bryant, to stick with football. Bryant's first love was baseball, and he told Henderson he wanted to quit football to concentrate on baseball.

Henderson opted for psychology. He gave him an ultimatum. He gently reminded him he was also the baseball coach.

Bryant agreed to play football, and was named the team's best offensive player that season. He received a scholarship to South Carolina, was named the outstanding athlete in the Atlantic Coast Conference and played 14 seasons as an All-Pro defensive back with the Minnesota Vikings, including four trips to the Super Bowl. (He missed two of those games because of injuries.)

"Coach Henderson was a tremendous motivator," said Wayne "Buffalo" Johnson, an offensive tackle. "Bobby Bryant was a great athlete, but we didn't have a lot of other great athletes. He had a way of making you play above your ability."

The 1963 season was marked by shutout victories over LaGrange (7-0) and Valdosta (13-0). It would be the start of six straight wins over LaGrange and three straight wins over the Wildcats. The Rams also won for the fourth straight year over Lanier, another one-point decision (14-13).

One of the losses in a 6-2-2 season came against Baker in Columbus. Baker was ahead 23-0 when Henderson pulled the starters and put his entire sophomore team in the game. The sophomores scored and, even though the Rams lost 23-7, it provided a bounce in the step of the team's younger players.

"The vast majority of them didn't play that much," said Henderson. "If it rained, some of their parents didn't even show up for the games. Derrell Parker was one of those players, and he scored the touchdown. I challenged the team to an early practice the next morning. I'll never forget Parker's father showing up, sitting in a lawn chair, and smoking a big cigar. He was proud of that touchdown."

The 1963 season was also marked by a tragic accident. A promising sophomore athlete named Johnny Higdon was climbing a tree to retrieve a kite for his brother, and he fell headfirst to the ground. He stayed in a coma for several months. The accident left him physically and mentally impaired.

He never played again. In his later years, he became a "spirit director" when the school was renamed Southwest. Henderson was inspired to call him the "greatest high school sports fan in America." (In 1988, he was awarded the "Macon's Telegraph's" annual Sam Burke Award for sportsmanship and service.)

A gifted class of sophomores began to get more playing time as the season progressed. In the next-to-last game against Moultrie, senior quarterback and co-captain Terry Colson got hurt and had to leave the game. Henderson had no choice but to put his second-string quarterback into the game.

It was a young sophomore named William Bradford Henderson, Jr. It was Billy's kid.

"He had come down with a stomach virus that week, but I had to play him anyway," Henderson said.

Brad led the Rams down the field on an 80-yard drive, completing 8-of-9 passes, including a touchdown pass to Carlie McNeil.

As a backup, he finished the year completing 34 of 72 passes for 632 yards and eight touchdowns.

By the next season, there was no doubt.

Brad Henderson would be Willingham's starting quarterback.

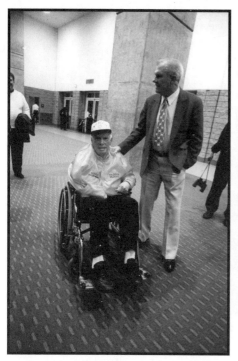

Henderson with legendary Valdosta coach Wright Bazemore at Georgia Dome in 1996. (Photo courtesy of Henderson family.)

Henderson with high school buddy Jesse Duckworth. (Photo courtesy of Henderson family.)

Henderson, top row and second from the right, with the Fitzgerald Pioneers baseball team in 1951. (Photo courtesy of Henderson family.)

Henderson returns kickoff against LSU in 1947. (Photo courtesy of Georgia Athletic Department.)

Henderson with son Brad in 1964. (Photo courtesy of Henderson family.)

Henderson meets with Clarke Central's "Breakfast Club." From right: Leroy Dukes, Henderson, Zippy Morocco and Don Perno. (Photo courtesy of Wingate Downs.)

Henderson eats a pre-game meal in peace at his home, with the telephone off the hook. (Photo courtesy of Wingate Downs.)

Lanier High School Coach John "Stooge" Davis. (Photo courtesy of Gena Wages.)

Henderson shares pregame talk with Clarke Central player Lacey Degnan in 1991. (Photo courtesy of Wingate Downs.)

Henderson with daughters (from left) Fran, Chris, and Carol in 1995. (Photo courtesy of Henderson family.)

Fosky reads story to Henderson children. (L-R) Brad, Carol, Chris, Johnny and Fran. (Photo courtesy of Henderson family.)

Henderson with Georgia football coach Wally Butts, left, and Georgia baseball coach Jim Whatley after signing with Macon Peaches in 1950.

Henderson with Athens High players Fran Tarkenton (10) and Bobby Towns (37) in 1954. (Photo courtesy of "Atlanta Journal-Constitution.")

Henderson was one of Georgia's all-time greats in baseball. (Photo courtesy of Georgia Athletic Department.)

Henderson started the football program at Willingham in 1958. (Photo courtesy of Henderson family.)

Henderson with coaching friend
Carol Bufford at Jefferson High
in 1952. (Photo courtesy of
Henderson family.)

Henderson visits graves of
his mother, Jewell, and son,
Brad, at Macon Memorial Park
in September 2004. (Photo
courtesy of Robert Seay.)

Henderson on sidelines at Clarke Central game. (Photo courtesy of Wingate Downs.)

Henderson huddles with Clarke Central players at practice. (Photo courtesy of Wingate Downs.)

East squad at the All-American Boys Baseball Game at Polo Grounds in New York in August 1945. Henderson is top row, fourth from left. To right of Henderson is Carl Hubbell and Babe Ruth. (Photo courtesy of Henderson family.)

Henderson hams it up for cameras at Clarke Central event. (Photo courtesy of Wingate Downs.)

Henderson meditates before Clarke Central game in 1991. (Photo courtesy of Wingate Downs.)

Henderson yells instruction to Clarke Central team. (Photo courtesy of "Athens Banner Herald.")

Henderson with WSB-TV camera man Duane Hardin.
(Photo courtesy of Wingate Downs.)

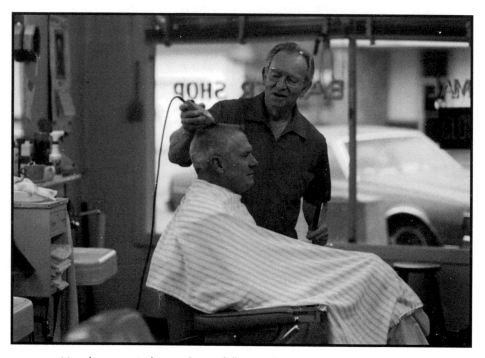

Henderson gets his traditional flat-top haircut from Athens barber
Andy Anderson. (Photo courtesy of Wingate Downs.)

Brad Henderson loved life and lived it to the fullest. (Photo courtesy of Henderson family.)

BRAD

Brad Henderson was born with a ball in his hands. It was as if the word "athlete" was printed beside his name on his birth certificate. X's and O's must have been the first two letters of the alphabet he learned.

He arrived in the world on a hot August day in 1948 while his dad was playing for Wrightsville in the Ogeechee League. It was a few weeks before Billy Henderson was set to begin his junior football season at Georgia.

By the time he was 2, his father was already working with him with a bat and ball. By the time he was 3, he was hanging out on the sidelines at Jefferson High football games.

When his father left to join the staff at Athens High, the young Henderson was introduced to one of his father's players, Fran Tarkenton. Tarkenton became one of his heroes. Later, astronaut John Glenn and President John F. Kennedy became his heroes, too.

As his father took college coaching jobs at Furman and South Carolina, Brad hung around the athletic departments. He was a football brat and gym rat. Beneath the glass on his desk, Henderson kept a photograph of a 7-year-old Brad, wearing a Furman baseball uniform in a "perfect batting stance."

He was not only a gifted athlete, he exuded confidence at an early age. When he was 12, while playing baseball for Macon Little League, one of his coaches during recess at Joseph N. Neel School explained that a runner at second base was considered to be in "scoring position."

"Coach," Brad interrupted, "whenever I'm at the plate, I'm in scoring position."

That same year, he hit .564, set a new state Little League record with 17 home runs (including two grand slams) in 25 games and played third base, second base, left field and catcher. As a pitcher, he was 8-0 and Macon won the state Little League championship.

The year before, as an 11-year-old in 1960, he had struck out with a runner in scoring position, to make the last out in the finals of the Little League state tournament. He collapsed at home plate, crying, but did not carry his disappointment for long. Twenty minutes later, he was eating a hamburger, counting the days until the start of football season.

His baseball skills were extraordinary, just like his dad. His sophomore year at Willingham, he batted .357. And some claim basketball may have been his best sport. He averaged 21 points per game for Willingham's "B" team in 1963-64.

Of course, he was best known for football. The coach's kid. The budding star.

"No doubt he was going to be a great athlete, just like Coach Henderson had been," said Wayne "Buffalo" Johnson, captain of the 1964 team. "He looked the part. He looked like his dad, right down to the crew cut."

But as much as he is remembered as an excellent player, he was an even better son, brother and friend.

"There was something about his heart that drew people in," said his sister, Fran Hobbs. "He was cute, so natural with people. He had a light. When he would smile, I would melt. My girlfriends would melt, too.

"And he was so protective. There wasn't a mean bone in his body, but I remember one day at the bowling alley some guys were trying to pull on my dress. Brad got very upset and told them to keep their hands to themselves. They backed off and walked away. Girls loved that. He made them feel so safe."

The Rams of 1964 returned 20 lettermen and an abundance of depth. On opening night of football season – Friday, Sept. 4, 1964 – Brad set a Willingham school passing record with 173 yards and two touchdowns in a 25-0 victory over Warner Robins. The opposing quarterback for the Demons that night was Sonny Perdue, who was elected governor of Georgia in 2002.

On Sunday night after the opening game, Fran was sitting on the front porch of the family's home at 1465 Westbury Drive. Brad came out and started talking to her. He was 16. She was 12.

"He was really interested in me," Fran said. "He wanted to know what I wanted to be when I grew up. He told me he wanted to be a dentist. He also told me I was a good sister, and he loved me very much."

The following Monday was Labor Day. The team watched game film that morning. Henderson gave his players the rest of the morning and early afternoon off. They were to report to practice later in the day.

Brad returned to the house. Fosky was in the back yard, hanging clothes on the clothes line. She always took great pride in cleaning his uniform. She even took an old toothbrush and cleaned his cleats.

Another sister, Carol Brooks, was 10 years old at the time. She remembers Brad telling Fosky he was picking up his girlfriend, Diane Driggars, and going with some friends on a picnic to High Falls State Park. He kissed his mother on the cheek, and left.

"As he was leaving, I remember my mother saying to me: 'Doesn't he look so handsome?'" Carol said.

Brad had turned 16 and gotten his driver's license just three weeks earlier. He appeared at the door of the coach's office and asked Henderson for the keys to the family's Ford Falcon station wagon. Henderson tossed him the keys and told him he needed to be back at the house by 3, so they could ride over to the school together.

When Brad failed to show up, Henderson walked the few blocks from Westbury to Canterbury. It was uncharacteristic of Brad to be late. Henderson was concerned, but not worried.

Assistant coach Mike Garvin had been the last to see Brad leave that day. He said a few words to him as Brad walked out of the gym. Later in the afternoon, Garvin had made a trip to K Mart on Riverside Drive. As he was driving up Ingleside, he heard an ambulance behind him on Riverside.

He was dating his future wife, Carolyn, at the time. They both looked back and saw the ambulance pass by. He dropped off Carolyn at her house, then was heading back to Willingham when he heard on the radio two teenagers had been killed in a wreck on Riverside Drive.

When Garvin returned to Willingham, he walked in the door of the coach's office and told Henderson about the accident.

Deep inside, intuition took over. Henderson knew it had to be Brad.

"Brad is never late," Henderson said.

On their way back to Macon, Brad and Diane were at a stop sign at Wesleyan Drive and Riverside. A speeding car driven by a 62-year-old Macon man hit them head on. Brad and Diane were killed instantly. The driver of the other car, who was drunk, died, too.

Then Sheriff Ray Wilkes showed up at the door. "He didn't have to say a word," Henderson said.

He went to the house and got Fosky. They rode with Wilkes to the hospital, where the halls were lined with people. Henderson was in shock.

Overcome with grief, he pulled back the sheet, and identified Brad.

When he returned home, the yard was full of people. Carol and Fran had been playing with some friends, Alicia and Constance Clance. Their mother, Barbara, drove Fran and Carol home.

"She was quiet. I knew in my heart something was wrong. I held Carol's hand," said Fran.

Said Carol: "I started counting cars a mile from home. I wondered why there were so many cars parked on the side of the road. I actually remember getting excited when I saw what seemed like hundreds of people in the front yard. I said, 'Look, we're having a party!' But, even at

10, I could tell something was terribly wrong."

Carol and Fran went downstairs to their parents' bedroom. Finally, Fosky broke the silence. "Brad and Diane have been in a wreck," she said.

"That's all she had to say," said Carol. "We all sat on their bed and cried for a long time."

The funeral was on Wednesday. They buried Diane that same day. After the service, the house was once again full of people. One was Georgia's new football coach, Vince Dooley, and Dean William Tate, UGA's dean of students. Henderson's longtime coaching friend, Johnny Griffith, was there, too.

"I knew I had to leave," Henderson said. "I had a lot to do. We had practice that afternoon. The team was my responsibility. I knew where I needed to be."

When he left the house to walk to the practice field, his sister, Doris, asked: "Where are you going?"

"Leave him alone," said Griffith. "This is what he needs to do."

It was Henderson's way of letting his players and coaching staff know that life goes on, no matter how heavy the heart. Still, it was difficult for the young people at both Willingham and McEvoy to come to grips with the deaths of two popular students.

"It was the first time I had ever had to deal with the death of a friend," said Cecil Bentley, one of Brad's close friends. "I cried and blubbered like most of the student body. Their deaths just made no sense. It scared me to think that we needed no reason to die and that we had no right to be alive."

Said Fran: "Brad was the most important person in my life. I looked up to him and wanted to be just like him. I hope I have a little bit of him in me."

Henderson later told the students that Brad and Diane lived 16 years and it gave him peace they had both accepted Christ at an early age.

"They both were happy," he said. "In fact, neither one of them could have been any happier. Brad lived life to the ultimate. He loved his family, his school, and he loved sports with a passion."

He remembers Diane being "pretty inside and outside."

"She used to caddy for Brad when he played golf," Henderson said. "In early August, we went to play at Riverside Golf and Country Club. It started raining, but we continued to play. I'll never forget Diane. Here was this beautiful girl, and her wet hair was all in her face. But she wasn't concerned about it. She always had a smile on her face."

Bentley said a Labor Day hasn't passed since 1964 that he has not thought of Brad.

"Usually he's there in my dreams, a cocky grin spread on his face and eyes burning with ideas that only a 16-year-old on top of the world could understand," he said. "You knew Brad was going places back then. He would someday play third base for the Dodgers, do shaving cream commercials on TV and maybe even manage a chain of restaurants or clothing stores in the off-season. ..."

In the weeks after Brad's death, Fosky sent a sympathy card to the family of the drunk driver. Henderson sat down and wrote a letter to his son in heaven:

Dear Brad:

A week has passed since your fatal accident and since that time I have had a tremendous urge to write this letter. This urge was brought about as I looked through your desk last Monday night viewing several of the letters I had written to you in previous years.

As I sat in your room, Brad, my mind wandered back over the sixteen years that we were privileged to have you, and I must say that, from a Dad's standpoint, you gave me enough fond memories to last a lifetime. My thoughts first wandered back to the summer of 1948, just before you were born. You recall that I was playing semi-pro baseball in Wrightsville and, through necessity, Mother remained in Athens to ensure a safe birth for you. Your mother would get extremely upset with me when I would ask how Brad was doing, because she was afraid I would be disappointed if you happened to be a girl. You may recall me mentioning the fact that you were the only boy to have a complete outfit in football and baseball before you came into the world.

In the letter, Henderson recalled when he was playing minor-league baseball in Fitzgerald. Brad was 2 years old. He was driving him to a local swimming pool.

"All of a sudden you threw a towel over my face, and the next thing I knew our car had gone under a truck that had stopped for a traffic light. As the excited driver opened the door to check our condition, he found me with my arms around you which prevented you from being thrown against the dash board. I would have given life itself to have been in the car with you the other day to absorb any pain you may have suffered.

On Anthony Road, across the street from where Brad had hit all those home runs playing for Macon Little League four years earlier, they began constructing a new football stadium.

On Sept. 2, 1965 – almost one year to the day after Brad's death – the stadium was dedicated.

The city named it Brad Henderson Memorial Stadium.

Henderson family Christmas 1956. (Photo courtesy
of Henderson family.)

LIFE WITH FATHER

Tragedy may have taken his oldest child away, but Billy Henderson never stopped being a father.

At night, he would go to each of the bedrooms and spend time with his children. Chris, the youngest, was 4 years old when Brad died.

"I would go into her room, and she would say a prayer," said Henderson. "She would put her hands around my neck. I can still feel those little arms. Without hesitation, and through complete faith, she would say, 'God bless Diane and Brad up in heaven.'"

Henderson was always close to his children. Even though the demands of his job kept him away from home for many hours each day, he always made time for his family.

"He was very involved with all five of us," said Carol. "He would take us to the park. He would play in the back yard. He would get up and cook breakfast for us every morning while Mama made our lunches for school. We would have a devotional at the table – all seven of us. Everybody had a different day of the week.

"Everything was structured. There had to be a plan. Even if it was Saturday. And even if you were sick."

The Henderson breakfast menu hardly varied – eggs, bacon, sausage, grits and toast.

Perhaps he felt the need to be part of his children's lives more than most. His own father died when he was 8, leaving him with only the memories of the man everyone said he looked and acted like.

"I took my children everywhere," he said. "I was like a big, yellow school bus."

On Saturday mornings, Henderson gave his wife a much-needed "vacation" from the children.

"He piled us all in the car, and it was Mama's morning to have a break," Carol said. "Sometimes we looked like orphans when we came home. Our clothes didn't match. He dressed us with the wrong colors. We weren't wealthy, but I never felt that."

It was the same way for Fran who, as the second-oldest, understood the sacrifices her father made for his family.

He moonlighted, taking extra jobs to help supplement his income. He worked at a bowling alley, a skating rink, a local convenience store and even sold insurance.

"We were cared for, no matter what it took, with all those mouths to feed," said Fran. "He didn't make enough money in coaching, so he worked all those other jobs so our mom could stay home with us. We had what we needed, and that's all that mattered."

There were times when Henderson would go see his pastor and friend, the Rev. Jimmy Waters, about his financial struggles at home.

"He always quoted scripture about Christ providing for our needs," Henderson said.

On Saturdays, he often would take his kids to the Willingham gym. They would jump on the trampoline and swing on the rope. They would shoot basketball and play hide-and-seek in the locker rooms.

Sometimes, he would come out and play with them. Then, he would tell them he had some more work to do, then slip off and take care of some of his coaching duties.

On Thanksgiving, he would take them to see the traditional Georgia-Georgia Tech freshman game at Grant Field in Atlanta.

Before Christmas, the family would travel to Atlanta and shop at Rich's department store downtown.

"He would watch us," said Fran. "He would wait at the escalator while we bought something for Mama. That was his one big splurge every year."

After Brad died, Johnny was the only son. He grew up in the same environment his older brother had. As a youngster, he was always tagging along behind his dad, on his way to whichever sport was in season. At Willingham football games, he had his own uniform to wear on the sidelines.

"I was about 6 or 7 years old, and I remember going to a Willingham-Lanier basketball game," Johnny said. "At a critical point in the game, I walked up to my dad and asked him for a dime for a Coke."

Henderson told his son not to bother him during the game. Later, he caught Johnny on a stool in the locker room, taking money from a player's locker. He did not spare the rod.

(Johnny obviously learned his lesson. Years later, in a freshman English class at the University of Georgia, he made an "A" on his essay titled, "My Most Unforgettable Night.")

Chris remembers the family trips to Jekyll Island in the family's light-blue Plymouth station wagon.

"Johnny and I would fight over who would sit in the last row because there was a hole in the floorboard," she said. "Mama and Daddy never knew we would drag our feet. And we had to stop at gas stations in every town to put water in the radiator so the car wouldn't overheat. I still have visions of Daddy standing over a smoking car."

Through the years, Chris learned that although her dad could be more set in his ways than most fathers, he wasn't some old-fashioned "square."

Once, he rode the "Scream Machine" roller coaster with some of his players at Six Flags.

Said Chris: "All my friends loved and adored him."

Jewell Henderson. (Photo courtesy of Henderson family.)

JEWELL AND RED

The grave is on the slope of a hill at Macon Memorial Park, her final resting place in the shade of a tall pine tree.

Part of Billy Henderson is buried here, too.

"It gets easier with time," he said. "But the hurt is always there."

His mother, Jewell Henderson, died on March 9, 1962. Two years later, his oldest son, Brad, would join her beneath the pines.

His big brother, Red, is gone now, too. He died on Feb. 15, 1994.

Jewell and Red had both been with him from the beginning. They each had an enormous influence on his life.

His mother had always been there for him, making the kinds of loving sacrifices only a mother could make.

In her final years, she lived in a one-room apartment on Cleveland Avenue. The cancer was painful. She was only 61.

"I will always be grateful I could be with her in her last days and make her comfortable" he said. "I would go by every day. Even when she was in a coma, she could recognize my footsteps. I watched her take her last breath."

Not a day goes by in Henderson's life that he doesn't reflect on something his mother told him or taught him.

"She taught by example," he said. "I was blessed she was my mother. Every Christmas, she made me think of the less fortunate. I never considered us not being wealthy. She gave me more than wealth."

"My mother was the strongest influence in my life. Anything positive came from her. All my bad habits, I learned on my own. She read the Bible every day of her life."

James "Red" Henderson was a "work in progress" when Billy was growing up as his little brother. He, too, became a high school coach. But he took a very different path.

They were always close, even though four years separated them in age. But James, who carried the nickname "Red" like his late father, would also carry a curse. His short temper led to many fights. In fact, Billy can't remember a time when James wasn't in a fight with somebody. Somewhere. He never started a fight but he finished plenty of them.

Unfortunately, James was unable to channel his energy into athletics. He did play football for Lanier, but later dropped out of high school. A man named Horace Vandiver, a local attorney, took him under his wing and trained him to be a boxer, and he became one of the city's finest. He won the Southeast Golden Gloves Welterweight championship.

"He was so aggressive in the ring. The buzzer would sound before the bell, and he would stand up and sprint to the other side of the ring and knock the guy's head off before he had a chance to get off the stool," said Henderson. "He was a buzz saw."

Red Henderson joined the Army when he was 17 and was an MP in Brazil, transporting German soldiers back and forth to Africa during World War II. He also boxed in the military, winning the service heavyweight title. His claim to fame was knocking out the heavyweight champion of Brazil.

After finishing the service, he went to college, got his Master's degree from the University of Georgia and served as assistant to the president of Furman University.

Later in his life, he was a high school principal and responsible for starting the football program at Forsyth County High in Cumming.

"He was one of my heroes, too," said Henderson.

Henderson with sisters Kathryn (left) and Doris, and brother Red.
(Photo courtesy of Henderson family.)

Henderson celebrates victory with daughter Fran. (Photo courtesy of Henderson family.)

THE LONGEST YARDS

There are times when he looks back and wonders how he made it through it all.

He cried a river. He had difficulty going to sleep. The nightmare of Sept. 7 stalked him at every turn.

"I would wake up in the middle of the night, hoping it all hadn't happened," he said.

The day after Brad's funeral, the Rams played Dougherty of Albany in a Thursday night game at Porter Stadium.

Claudie Brown took over the quarterbacking duties. But, in the first half, he injured his knee. So Henderson brought pint-sized Jack Evans off the bench.

"He was 5-foot-8, weighed 140 pounds and ran the 100 in 30 minutes," Henderson said. "But, that night, he was 9 feet tall and ran the 100 in 9 seconds flat."

Dougherty's coach, John Duke, had been a teammate of Henderson's at Georgia.

"You would have assumed he would have had sympathy," Henderson said. "We won 28-6, and I went out to shake his hand after the game. He accused me of running up the score."

Competing in Region 1AAA, the Rams posted their best record in school history at 8-1-1, losing only to eventual state champion Columbus, 9-6, and battling to a 6-6 tie with Albany.

The 1965 team also ranked with the Willingham greats, finishing 7-1-2, and beating cross-town rival Lanier for the sixth straight year. But the pinnacle came when the Rams scored with 2:25 left in the game to knock off unbeaten and eventual state champion Valdosta, 12-7.

"Fosky led the cheers in the dressing room after the game," Henderson said. "I learned a lesson that night. Never celebrate until the season is over. The next week, Jordan whipped us 35-13."

Jordan's upset put Valdosta in the playoffs, and the Wildcats marched into the state championship game against Athens.

"It was like the Twilight Zone," Henderson said. "Wayne Bevill, Eddie Battle and I went up to see Athens High and Valdosta in the state championship game that year. Valdosta had a banner thanking Jordan for beating us."

The following year, the program hit a downward spiral. The Rams faltered to 4-5-1 in both 1966 and '67, losing to Lanier both years. Willingham went 5-5 in 1968 and '69.

Henderson was busy with other things. Along with Helen Faulkner and Ann Hadarits, two P.E. teachers at McEvoy, he organized "McWill Night." It was a night designed to promote fitness in the community. High school students from both schools, as well as several from the grammar schools, got to participate in front of thousands of people in attendance.

Henderson made sure it was successful. He recruited folks like Gov. Jimmy Carter, who went on to be elected President. Former governors Lester Maddox and Carl Sanders participated. So did Georgia head football coach Vince Dooley.

Designated as a fund-raiser for Willingham's athletic department, the first "McWill Night" was held at the Macon Coliseum in 1969. It involved more than 2,000 participants and more than 6,350 spectators. By the next year, the event grew to include youngsters from nine elementary schools.

It featured everything from jogging, calisthenics, swimming, rope climbing, weightlifting and tumbling.

Maddox, the colorful governor, rode his bicycle backward. And 82-year-old Gene Searcy, a legend at Macon's YMCA, stood on his head to entertain the crowd.

The event drew national coverage from Parade, a Sunday newspaper magazine, where Macon Mayor Ronnie "Machine Gun" Thompson called it "our once-a-year carnival of physical fitness."

At one point, Henderson made a public statement that Willingham students "were the most physically fit in the world."

Of course, a rebuttal came from across town.

"No. 1 in the world?" said Lanier Junior High principal Johnny Jones. "They're not even No. 1 in Macon."

No, the rivalry never stopped.

Henderson involved himself with other projects. It didn't seem to be enough that he was the athletic director at a large high school and coached two major sports. He started a gymnastics team at Willingham. He became head of the summer recreation programs for city schools.

He piled even more on an already full plate.

"I probably set a record for joining organizations in Macon," he said.

He volunteered for Big Brothers, Boy Scouts and the YMCA. He spoke to every civic club in town. He was a member of the building authority for the Macon Coliseum.

"I got involved to stay busy so I would come home at night so exhausted I could fall asleep," he said. "I was like a zombie. I spread myself too thin. My life was mechanical."

Looking back, he said he should have resigned after the 1965 season.

"I should have stepped down," he said. "We were mediocre, and I take full responsibility for that. I was grieving and didn't know it."

Meanwhile, the 1969 baseball season helped take off some of the edge. The Rams won the state baseball title.

"I was coming back to life," he said. "I remember one day I had on my baseball uniform. I had Fran, Carol, Johnny and Chris all in the car. They were going with me. I had the window down and came to a stop sign. I felt the sun shining on my face. I hadn't felt that way in a long time."

His sense of humor returned, too. In the Georgia High School Association All-Star baseball game that summer, he was told there would be "free substitution." So he inserted Terry Holder, of Evans High, in the leadoff spot. Holder hit three straight doubles to open the game at Atlanta-Fulton County Stadium. Each time, Henderson used a pinch-runner at second base, then put him back at the plate. GHSA officials quickly called an end to that strategy.

In Macon, the winds of change began to swirl. Integration was approaching in the public schools. It would require a major transition. Not only would segregation end and black schools would merge with white schools, but in Macon girls would begin attending classes with boys.

The names would change, too. Predominantly white schools such as Willingham, Lanier, Miller, McEvoy, Mark Smith and Lasseter would be combined with black schools Ballard-Hudson and Appling to form new schools called Central, Southwest and Northeast.

Henderson had been preparing for the change. He had been named athletic director at Southwest, a new school that combined students from Willingham and McEvoy with Ballard-Hudson. Ballard-Hudson was a black school that had produced such great athletes as John "Blue Moon" Odom, who pitched in the World Series for the Oakland A's, and NFL greats Jim Parker and Tommy Hart.

He paid a visit to all the feeder elementary schools to encourage participation in sports at the new school. He hired Don Richardson, the highly successful basketball coach at Ballard-Hudson Junior High, as the new head basketball coach at Southwest. It turned out to be a brilliant move. At Southwest, Richardson won six state titles and a national championship in 1978-79.

But, at a board of education meeting that spring, Henderson was not happy with what he heard. No matter where a male student lived in Macon, he could attend Central if he wanted to participate in the ROTC program.

However, Southwest would not have an ROTC program and could only draw students from within its own district. Henderson felt this gave Central an unfair advantage to recruit athletes county-wide. Henderson had a confrontation with Central Coach Goot Steiner at the meeting.

Driving home in the car that night with assistant coach Lloyd Bohannon, Henderson suddenly stopped his car on Canterbury Road, slammed his fist on the dash board and said: "That's it!!!"

Enough was enough.

"Reflecting back on it, it was the same sort of decision I had also made when I left Furman for the University of South Carolina. It was what I had to do based on principle," he said. "It was kind of like when I was playing baseball at 23 years old and telling myself I didn't have to do this any more. When I got back to Macon, the sea opened up and I went to Jefferson."

This time, he somehow sensed the school he had built, nurtured and poured 12 years of his life into would never be the same.

"I was born with Willingham, and I died with it," he said.

In his letter of resignation to school superintendent Julius Gholson, he recommended assistant Billy Beale be promoted to athletic director and Bohannon be elevated to head football coach.

He stayed the rest of the school year. He told local newspaper reporters he was weighing his job opportunities but had not made a decision.

"Those were the longest three months of my life," he said. "I was like a man without a country."

Henderson and Raymond Bateman, left, help injured quarterback Claudie Brown off the field. (Photo courtesy of "The Macon Telegraph.")

Henderson with son Johnny at Mount de Sales in 1972. (Photo courtesy of "The Macon Telegraph.")

"HALFTIME"

It was a time of Henderson's life Fosky would later refer to as "halftime."

Finding a job was not going to be a problem. Henderson told Harley Bowers, the longtime sports columnist for "The Macon Telegraph", he was entertaining several job offers.

One was from "Readers Digest" magazine. His duties would be to call on athletic groups for fund-raisers.

But everyone knew his heart was coaching. It wouldn't be long until he found his way back.

"After I resigned at Willingham, it was like all the blood left my body," he said. "I was like a mummy. It was as close a feeling to having a death in the family."

In 1959, Henderson had hired a young coach named Mike Garvin as an assistant. Garvin was named head coach at Mount de Sales in 1967 and, in 1970, had an opening for a baseball coach and assistant football coach.

Within a month after resigning at Willingham, Henderson was ready to jump back in. Garvin got a call from his former mentor. Henderson's resume' was a 64-42-14 record at Willingham in football. In 1969, his baseball Rams won the state AAA title.

"He told me he wanted to get back into coaching but he didn't want to leave Macon," said Garvin. "I'll be honest. I was apprehensive. I had worked for him, and now he would be working for me. I had difficulty imagining him as my assistant."

Garvin also didn't know if the school could afford the salary of someone with Henderson's experience. But he was able to work it out with school officials.

He was also able to work something else out.

"He was willing to accept me as a boss, and we helped each other," he said.

Of course, there were those who questioned Garvin's decision to hire his former boss. Many weren't sure it would work.

"You have to give him credit for being a secure person," Henderson said. "I was a better assistant this time around in my coaching career, because I knew exactly what he needed. We were very compatible because he had been on my staff."

Henderson laughed and said he had given Garvin more responsibility at age 22 than Garvin gave him at 42.

Garvin had always been grateful for the opportunity Henderson had given him to join the staff at Willingham in 1959. Garvin had been an accomplished coach at the elementary school level, taking Alexander IV to the Pony Bowl, which was once a Thanksgiving tradition in Macon.

He had been too small to play football at Lanier, but was greatly influenced by Coach Tom Porter, who was his algebra teacher. Garvin had a burning desire to join the staff at Lanier, but was only offered a job as a teacher.

He not only went on to become one of the city's most revered head football coaches but was regarded as one of the top math teachers in Macon.

Mount de Sales is a Catholic school in downtown Macon on Orange Street. Henderson used to walk by the school on the way to his house on Columbus Street.

He would look over at what he and the other children would call the "Mystic Wall." He could see the nuns in their habits. It was always very mysterious.

He interviewed for the coaching position with Sister Lourdes Sheehan. He was impressed with the way she handled herself and her school. He remembers looking down at her left hand and noticing a wedding band on her ring finger.

He asked her about it. He always thought nuns never married.

"I'm married to Christ," was her answer.

In many ways, the school was a perfect fit. Although small, it had most of the resources of a larger public school without many of the problems. Students had to follow the dress code. There was a code of conduct both at school and off-campus. The men faculty were required to wear ties.

"It was the way every school in the world should be," Henderson said.

Garvin often sought Henderson's advice. And he listened.

"I think it shows how secure Billy was in his coaching and teaching kids," said Melvin Kruger. "They complimented each other."

Kruger had been a close friend of Henderson's since their days at Lanier. His son, Steve, played on the Cavaliers team and was close friends with Johnny Henderson.

In 1970, Garvin began playing more of the younger players, including Johnny Henderson and Ben Zambiasi. It paid off, too. Johnny Henderson and Zambiasi led Mount de Sales to Class C state titles in 1970 and '71 and a Class A championship in 1973.

(Both went on to become defensive stars on Georgia's "Junkyard

Dogs" defenses of the mid-1970s. Henderson was drafted by the Chicago Cubs in the third round after his senior year of high school, but opted to sign a football scholarship with the Bulldogs, where he was an All-SEC performer. Zambiasi set a career record for tackles at Georgia. In 2004, he was inducted into the Canadian Football League Hall of Fame.)

As an assistant, Henderson demanded the same kind of discipline and hard work out of his players as he did as a head coach.

"He would work us so hard," remembered Johnny. "After practice, the other guys would come up to me and tell me they sure were glad they didn't have to go home with him."

Winning the football titles, as well as two state baseball championships, continued to energize Henderson. In 1972, after winning his second state championship in baseball at Mount de Sales, he was named the National High School Baseball Coach of the Year.

It marked only the second time a Georgia high school coach had been named national coach of the year in any sport. In 1970, Wright Bazemore of Valdosta was recognized for his accomplishments as a football coach.

Always looking for ways to maximize every minute of every day, Henderson involved himself in other things.

One of his favorite pastimes was playing competitive handball. He worked out a deal with Sister Lourdes that would allow him to play every day at lunch, even though it meant leaving campus. The following year, when Sister Fidelis Barragon became principal, he reminded her that time off to play handball during lunch was in his contract.

"I told her I wouldn't eat lunch. It was important that I play," he said. "So every day I would leave the school wearing a coat and tie and carrying a briefcase."

He would walk the six blocks to the Macon Health Club (the former YMCA). He would walk past Hart's Mortuary, where funeral director Joe Childs flagged him down one day.

"I've often wondered what you have in the briefcase," he said to Henderson.

Henderson placed the briefcase on the hood of a car and opened it. Inside were shoes, shorts, a T-shirt, handball gloves and a jock strap.

Some of his closest handball partners were Tommy Hulett, Bob Berlin, Hubert Howell and Claude Zigler.

"I loved it," he said. "I always wanted to play the best. I liked playing against the younger guys, too. It made me work harder."

In 1972, he played Berlin for the championship in the city tournament. The game was tied and, at match point, Berlin suddenly caught the ball and yelled, "You win!" He had called a foul on himself for hitting his own wrist.

"It was one of the best demonstrations of sportsmanship I've ever seen," Henderson said.

Also, he and longtime friend Jesse Duckworth opened Camp Pineworth on Lake Tobesofkee in 1972. It was a 58-acre camp for boys and girls.

Still, he knew it was time to start looking for new challenges. At age 44, he was restless.

Several schools had tried to lure him away. LaGrange, Cochran (Bleckley County) and Dublin all put out feelers to test his interest. He turned them all down.

He was reading in the newspaper about how Weyman Sellers, his old boss at Athens High School, had been going through some rough sledding at the new Clarke Central High in Athens.

Sellers was one of the state's winningest high school coaches, and had enjoyed success as recently as 1969, when Athens High tied Valdosta for the state title.

Clarke Central was the merger of Athens High and the black school, Burney Harris. It was not a smooth transition.

"There were a lot of racial things going on," Henderson said. "I called Weyman to reassure him things were going to work out and asked if there was anything I could do."

It wasn't long after that Henderson learned Sellers had been dismissed. So he called him back to let him know he was going to apply for the vacant job. Because of their long friendship, he didn't want Sellers to find out about it second-hand.

Henderson then called John Tilliski, the assistant principal at Clarke and his former teammate at UGA. Tilliski said he would talk to Don Hight, the principal, to see if there was any interest. Hight set up an interview in January 1973.

At least two other veteran high school coaches had expressed interest in the job – Jim Hughes of Colquitt County in Moultrie and former Thomson High coach Paul LeRoy.

But Henderson emerged as the leading candidate.

"They later said they didn't interview me – I interviewed them," Henderson said.

At Mount de Sales, the nuns got together and prayed he would either reject the job or that he wouldn't be offered the job.

It wasn't long before they believed their prayers had been answered.

Henderson told Clarke Central thanks – but no thanks.

There were plenty of issues for Henderson to consider when he was weighing his own interest. There had been opportunities to join Georgia's coaching staff in the past, but each time he turned the offer down.

"My children didn't want to move, and I thought it was important for Fosky to be able to visit Brad's grave every day," he said. "So I could always blame it on them."

He spent the next two weeks going back and forth on his decision to accept the job if it was still available. One of his former Athens High players, Dallas Tarkenton, the older brother of Fran Tarkenton, called on behalf of Clarke Central to let him know they could use a man of his caliber and credentials.

One night, he was sitting in his chair in the living room, when he decided to call Hight to see if the position was still open. He was going to tell him he had reconsidered and was ready to commit.

"I took three steps toward the phone before it rang," he said. "It was Mr. Hight. I told him if he had waited another minute, he could have saved himself some money on a long-distance phone call."

Henderson told him he had a change of heart. He was ready to throw his hat back in the ring if the job was still open.

He hung up the phone and called Fosky, Fran, Carol, Johnny and Chris into the living room.

"I'm going to Athens," he said. "You can either join me now or join me later. But I've got to go."

He expected a challenge from his family. Not a word was spoken.

Fran was already working and Carol was at Georgia Southern. Fosky and Chris joined Henderson in Athens in January 1974. It was decided Johnny would finish his senior year at Mount de Sales. He lived with his aunt and uncle, Jack and Raye Lane, then with the Kruger family.

Henderson was anxious to start. He had to assemble a staff and start talking to potential players.

But the nuns at Mount de Sales told him not so fast. He would need to finish his contract for the academic school year.

So he commuted back and forth after the start of Clarke Central's spring practice on May 1.

He was ready to be a head football coach again.

Henderson took over a Clarke Central program that was divided in
1973. (Photo courtesy of Wingate Downs.)

'Wouldn't Be In Your Shoes'

Henderson had been called a lot of things during his coaching career. This time, there seemed to be a unified voice.

"Crazy" was the adjective most often used.

Why would anyone want to take the reins of a program torn apart by racial strife, where support and participation were lacking and the athletic department had a sizeable debt. There were only 19 players left on the team after the disastrous 1972 season.

Sam Burke, the executive secretary of the Georgia High School Association, told Henderson he questioned his sanity.

"He wasn't the only one," Henderson said. "A lot of people advised me not to go to Clarke Central."

He even got sympathy cards in the mail.

"There was a lot of bitterness," he said. "Both black and white students were clinging to the past. Clarke Central was just a building, and the students there had no tradition, no common background."

Hight had been assistant principal at Athens High in the 1960s and had come back as principal in 1970.

In 1969, Athens had tied Valdosta for the state AAA championship behind quarterback Andy Johnson.

"We tied Valdosta. We thought we had won, and they thought they had lost," Hight said. "But three years after we won the state title, the team had dwindled to just 19 players. We went from winning a state championship to winning just one game. Tensions were high and morale was low."

So the change was made. Hight believed Henderson was the right man for the job. So did Charles McDaniel, the county's school superintendent who later became state school superintendent.

"Billy had the charisma for the job," said Hight. "We wanted somebody who could bring the community together, both black and white, and heal the wounds. We knew he couldn't turn it around immediately. It would take time. He also had a very green team. But people looked at him as a hero. He did not see color. He was a fair man."

That spring, Henderson called a meeting for all young men interested in playing football. He drove to the school, parked near the gym and got out of his car.

"There was a crowd of students standing around, and they noticed me," Henderson said. "A lot of the boys had long hair and facial hair – two things I associated with war protesters and burning the American flag. They took one look at me and one of them said: 'Oh, my God!'

"And I said: 'Look, you don't bother mine, and I won't bother yours'. I remembered back at Willingham in 1966, I had gotten two barber chairs before the beginning of the season, and I made the players line up and get all their hair shaved off. One of my players, Wayne Jones, looked like he was about to cry. He said: 'Coach, I'll get my hair cut, but it won't make me a better football player.' I always remembered that."

Many of the returning players wondered about their new coach's staying power. One player, Chuck Conley, who went on to become a high school football coach himself, told quarterback Doug Henson, "Don't worry, he won't last a week."

Still, some quit the team and others transferred to cross-town rival Cedar Shoals. Some parents had enrolled their children in local private schools.

Jeff Turk was one of them. His parents, Ray and Demaris Turk, had enrolled him at Athens Academy, even though the school had no sports program at the time.

It was especially painful for Demaris, who had known Billy and Fosky Henderson when she was a student at Athens High in the 1950s.

"Things had hit rock-bottom at Clarke Central," she said. "Those were some rough years. There was a lot of turmoil. The adjustment was difficult. And it wasn't just because of integration. The tradition was gone."

But she knew if there was one man who could turn it around, it was Henderson. Her son, Jeff, transferred to Clarke Central and was a ninth-grader on Henderson's first team in 1973.

To convince others to join the fold, Henderson reverted to his grass-roots approach. He went to all of Clarke Central's feeder elementary and middle schools. He talked to students. He showed movies about the positive aspects of playing football. He sent out fliers. He put up posters. He knocked on doors.

Seeking some advice, he asked one of the principals, William McBride, what he would do if he were in his shoes.

"Lord Jesus!" McBride said, "I wouldn't be in your shoes!"

Morale and school spirit had reached low ebb. The former Athens High players walked around the halls in their letter jackets, and Burney

Harris athletes wore their own letter jackets. Henderson remembers standing in the gym at a pep rally and watching the cheerleaders do their routine: "Two bits! Four bits! Six bits! A dollar! All for Clarke Central stand up and holler."

"I counted 'em," he said. "Three people stood up. I told those folks I hoped I lived to see the day when everybody would stand up and be proud of this school."

There wasn't any grass on their home field, and the players had to paint their own helmets. But whenever and wherever he met resistance, Henderson remembered the sign on the wall of the Lanier gym when he was 13 years old.

It Can Be Done.

He adopted it as the official motto of the Clarke Central athletic department.

"I was ready to be a head coach again," he said. "I had a plan. It was just a matter of executing that plan. I was grateful for the opportunity. I felt like I had been given a second chance. I would get to the school every morning at 3 or 4 a.m. There just weren't enough hours in the day."

He was confident he could bring the divided factions together. McDaniel and Hight, also were convinced he could heal the ugly scars of the past.

"I called him 'Mr. Sunshine,'" said Billy Harper, a veteran sports writer for "The Athens Banner Herald and Daily News." "He was always so cheerful. He was a great healer of wounds. And that was good, because there were plenty of them."

Henderson managed to attract 100 boys for spring practice in May. He had the locker rooms painted and the weight room restored (it had been turned into a storage room for the gymnastics team.) He started a running program.

He established a six-step program, designed to involve the administration, faculty, parents and community. He organized an informal group of Clarke Central boosters and gave them both a name – "The Breakfast Club" – and responsibility for being a force for positive change. Among the regulars were Mayor Julius Bishop, Zippy Morocco, Judge Joe Gaines, Mayor Lauren Coile, A. B. Weathersby, Ray Turk, Brack Rowe, Dick Payne, Bill Osborn, Doug Henson Sr., Bill Hudgins, Norman Johnson, Bernie Johnson, Jim Tardy, James Carter, Anna and Reese Conley, Clyde Harris, Nate Williams and Leroy Dukes.

He also was connecting with his players in ways only Billy Henderson could connect. He did have a way with words.

Ricky Smith was a ninth grader when Henderson gave one of his early locker room speeches.

"I'll never forget it," said Smith, now a football coach at Athens Christian. "He said the first thing he wanted us to know was that he was prejudiced. I looked around the room. He said he was prejudiced for people who tried, people who cared and people who worked together."

It wasn't long before almost everything Henderson said was the gospel.

"He made you accountable," said Smith. "He made you play hard and go to church. He instilled values in you. He could have told me to jump off a cliff, and I would have."

Henderson went to Hight and told him he wanted to take the team to Jekyll Island for preseason football camp. He wanted to revive the tradition he had begun at Willingham.

"He (Hight) asked who would pay for it. The school had no money for anything like that," Henderson said. "I told him the kids would pay. We had boys on the team who couldn't afford to pay, so we got them jobs for the summer. They were able to pay their own way. It gave them a sense of pride that they were able to do that."

He met with parents and showed films of the Jekyll Island camps he held when he was at Willingham.

"I told them it was invaluable. We would sleep, hurt, eat, cry and become one," he said. "There was no way to measure the value of that camp."

The Gladiators attended camp in August that year and began preparing for their opening game against Central-Macon. The Rev. Jimmy Waters, Henderson's former pastor at Mabel White Baptist Church in Macon, gave the pregame devotional for Clarke Central.

Doug Henson, the Gladiators' starting quarterback, got knocked out cold on the opening kickoff. Central-Macon won the game 41-20. Henderson, the eternal optimist, was quoted in the newspaper the next day as saying: "We would have won the game if we had more time."

To which Central-Macon coach Gene Brodie responded: "Yeah, and if a bullfrog had wings he wouldn't have a bruised tail."

Clarke finished 4-6 that year. But, included in those victories were wins over Griffin and Statesboro. Things were so tight with the athletic department's budget that Henderson had to borrow some jerseys and equipment from Gainesville High just to get the through the season. Gainesville's coach was Bobby Gruhn, yet another one of Henderson's old Lanier teammates.

"We weren't world beaters," Henderson said. "We even celebrated first downs. But we put the smiles back on the students' faces. There was some expectancy. People could see hope."

The biggest sacrifice Henderson had to make was not being able to coach his son, Johnny, who was quarterbacking Mount de Sales to another state title. Henderson was, however, able to keep up with his son's accomplishments and attend several playoff games.

By season's end, Clarke's athletic department deficit had been significantly reduced, partly through the sale of season tickets and other fund-raisers. Pride was restored. There was a beautification effort on campus. Flowers were planted in the area around the pine trees on the hill in the end zone.

"Our theme was that you shouldn't curse the darkness," Henderson said. "You should turn on some lights."

Another decision by Henderson to help unite the community was playing the annual spring game in honor of the late Cobern Kelley. Kelley, who died in 1968, had a profound impact on many of the young people in Athens in his position as youth director at the YMCA.

Henderson made the spring game much more than that. It was a day that involved the entire school, with activities and competition by P.E. classes, intramurals and participation in everything from track to volleyball to gymnastics to soccer.

By 1974, the Gladiators had established a winning record at 5-4-1 . Henderson won despite investing in a youth movement, playing several sophomores and a few freshmen.

"I didn't just throw my seniors away," he said. "We were building a good team. I knew by the '75 season we would be ready."

It didn't start out that way. The Gladiators opened the '75 season losing to Wheeler 19-0. Then came a 54-6 thumping at the hands of Warner Robins, a team that was on the brink of going undefeated and being crowned mythical national champions the following year.

"They looked like a college team out there," recalled Demaris Turk. "They killed us."

On the third week of the '75 season, the Gladiators went to Gainesville and lost 28-0.

In their first three games, they had been outscored 100-6.

"Fosky was the first person I saw when I came off the field after the Gainesville game," said Henderson. "She asked me what in the world I was doing. I just looked at her."

He called his team together after the game.

"I told them our effort was unacceptable and that it was my responsibility to see that they performed to the maximum," he said. "I called a practice for 7 a.m. the next morning. I suggested they stay home because I was going to try to kill them. All but one player showed up."

Dave Williams, a reserve quarterback, remembers one of Henderson's fiery locker-room speeches. The coach kicked a helmet across the floor.

There was stunned silence.

"I just broke my toe," said a red-faced Henderson, "and I don't care."

The Gladiators returned to fundamental football. The players drew closer and began to come together as a team. The next game was against cross-town rival Cedar Shoals. Although they lost 21-0 to a very good Jaguar team, Henderson was encouraged by their improvement.

By the next week, the Gladiators had proclaimed it a "new season" with their first Region 8AAA game. They shocked undefeated and fourth-ranked Dunwoody, 14-7, for their first victory of the season.

Before the game, Henderson had one of the school's custodians, Harvey Day, mount a white horse dressed in gladiator's armor. That was the impetus for six straight wins and sub-region championship.

"The 1975 team is very close to my heart," Henderson said. "What they accomplished was the result of hard work, faith, perseverance and a tremendous amount of character on the part of our football players. These people experienced hardship, defeat, ridicule and had every reason in the world to get discouraged."

They followed the 6-5 season with a 9-2 mark in 1976. The hard work and commitment had begun to pay dividends.

By 1977, Henderson and his staff knew they had assembled a team that could possibly compete for a state championship.

Then tragedy struck.

The team had gone to Jekyll Island for its summer camp. Following Thursday's intrasquad game, often known as the Golden Isles Bowl, Henderson had always given players an option of staying an extra day with their families who had come down to watch the game. He returned to Athens with the other players, following in a van with Fosky, the quarterbacks and managers.

Just outside of Greensboro, he and Fosky heard on the radio a Clarke Central football player had been killed by lightning at Jekyll Island.

Barry Malcolm was an offensive guard who weighed 150 pounds and "had a heart as big as the world," Henderson said. In tackling drills, he didn't mind taking on the biggest player he could find.

He had stayed behind with his parents to enjoy a few days at Jekyll. Not long after the buses had left, he was talking to his brother, Chuck, near the steps leading to the beach. It was a hazy day. All of a sudden, a lightning bolt came out of nowhere.

Henderson stopped the van and had the three team buses pull over. He got on each bus and told the players the news. By the time the buses reached the school, a large crowd had gathered.

His daughter, Fran, was a nurse at St. Mary's Hospital in Athens. She was at the school when Henderson and the team arrived.

"He waited until every player had a ride home," she said. "Then he went behind the school and cried. It just killed him. He loved those players like they were his own children. He loved them from the bottom of his toes. I don't think he blamed himself. It just hurt him. I think he felt like it was Brad all over again."

Henderson had known Barry as an eighth-grader. He was always volunteering in any way he could to help the program, even if it meant cleaning the gym.

The Clarke Central players had Barry's No. 65 sewn on their jerseys and dedicated the season to their fallen teammate. Clarke Central's weight room was dedicated to him the following season. (The gym is co-dedicated to the late Dr. Jack McDonald, the team physician.)

"You can't imagine the shock and numbness unless you have been there," Henderson said. "I thought about Barry's parents and brother having to make that long, lonely drive from Jekyll back to Athens.

"I had talked to my teams about Brad down through the years. There were times when a lot of these players came to my house. After Barry's death, they all wanted to be together."

At Clarke Central, Henderson won three state football titles and made the playoffs 18 straight years. (Photo courtesy of Wingate Downs.)

HEART OF A CHAMPION

Henderson's five-year plan had reached its fifth year. He had taken over a program that had hit bottom and was climbing to the top of a great mountain.

"What he did here was magic," said his daughter, Carol. "He got people working together. He had this ability to do that. People were attracted to him. They were fascinated with him."

He had told those pioneer players they could learn a lot about life through athletics.

"In athletics, as in life, you're going to get knocked down and you have to learn to cope with it," he said.

A week before the 1977 season opener against Cedar Shoals, the Gladiators were reeling from the death of a popular player. It wasn't the first Henderson team that had to learn to play with a heavy heart beneath those shoulder pads.

Clarke did not have a stockpile of great athletes. At best, this was a makeshift team where all the pieces seemed to fit. A converted quarterback. An offensive lineman kicking. And a defensive lineman punting. But it all worked.

The Gladiators beat Cedar Shoals 7-0, the first of what would become a remarkable seven shutouts in the Gladiators' 10-game regular season. Clarke had outscored its opponents 211-25 heading into the first round of the playoffs.

One by one, the playoff opponents fell: Lakeside (16-14), Newnan (14-7) and Southwest DeKalb (20-7). Then came the state title game against Valdosta, in a battle of two unbeaten teams.

It is best remembered as a marquee matchup between two big-name quarterbacks: Clarke Central's Jim Bob Harris, who went to Alabama, and Valdosta's Buck Belue, who signed with Georgia. The Wildcats had a chance to win late in the game, but missed a 31-yard field-goal attempt with 1:23 left.

Clarke won the game, 16-14, and Henderson had won his first state championship as a head football coach.

He had been part of two state titles in football as an assistant coach at Mount de Sales. He had won two state baseball titles at Mount de Sales and a baseball crown at Willingham. And, lest we forget, that swimming state championship at Athens High.

But this was incomparable.

"I'll never forget it," he said.

He will also never forget what took place just a few days before the championship game, on a Thanksgiving Day in the team's weight room.

He remembers it as "one of my most treasured moments in coaching."

A young man named Mike Walston, who was the youth minister at Beech Haven Baptist Church, was asked to lead the team in a devotional and prayer.

"We had mamas and dads, friends and girlfriends. It was wall-to-wall humanity," Henderson said. "When we all held hands, I could literally see hands shaking. Every head was bowed. It was a beautiful moment. Black hands were holding white hands. Rich hands were holding poor hands. Every walk of life was represented in that room, holding hands and working for a common purpose. It always stuck with me how great it could be if the whole world could be like that."

Winning seasons and trips to the playoffs soon became as common as Henderson's weekly trips to Five Points Barber Shop, where he got his famous crew cuts from barbers Andy Anderson and Herschel Reeves.

The summer before the 1978 season was long and involved. Fosky had been having back problems and was diagnosed with scoliosis. A doctor in Atlanta referred her to a top doctor in Minneapolis.

"We went up to meet with him and, when he walked in with all his assistants, he looked like Bear Bryant," Henderson said.

Fosky had three different operations – each lasting nine hours – over a period of three months. Fortunately, she had a sister, Madelyn Zollars, who lived in Minneapolis and was able to stay with her.

When Henderson went for visits, he often went to the Minnesota Vikings training camp. He had two former players on the Vikings roster – Fran Tarkenton and Bobby Bryant.

But it was another pro football player who commanded Henderson's interest. After three years as a vital member of the Georgia defense, Johnny was trying to make the Baltimore Colts as a free agent. He made it to the final cut before he was released.

"It was very hard for me to tell Fosky," Henderson said. "She was lying there in bed, with tears streaming down her face. She knew how much it meant to him."

Henderson was able to attend football camp at Jekyll Island with the team the week following Fosky's final surgery. She had to wear a cast for one year.

The 1978 team finished 9-2, losing to Cedar Shoals, 12-3, early in the season and dropping a 17-15 game to Lakeside in the region championship game. But, in 1979, the Gladiators were right back in the championship hunt, finishing 15-0 and beating Tift County 20-10 in the title game on a frozen field at Death Valley in Athens behind quarterback Charlie Dean. The Tift County team was coached by Gene Brodie, a Goot Steiner disciple who had won the 1975 state title as head coach at Central-Macon.

It was that same year Henderson awoke to newspaper headlines that he was a candidate for the Georgia Tech job. He did interview for the job, but later emphasized he had no real interest in returning to college coaching. He truly loved working with young men in high school. Tech hired one of its former players, Bill Curry.

The success of the late 1970s had carried over into the early 1980s. The Gladiators went into every season with high expectations. Anything less than a state championship meant they had fallen short of their goal.

In 1980, the Gladiators posted a 9-3 record and were knocked out in the region championship game by another close score, 14-13 to Peachtree. A 7-4 season in 1981 was followed by a 12-1 mark in 1982, again falling in the playoffs in a one-point loss, this time a 7-6 defeat to Griffin in the area championship game.

For the most part, Clarke was able to handle life in the upper echelon of high school football in Georgia. In 1983, the Gladiators annihilated their first 12 opponents by a combined score of 409-22. Included in that impressive showing were eight shutouts, including six in a row.

For any of the disbelievers, longtime Clarke camera man Bob Molleur was there to capture it on the highlight reel.

Soon, Clarke Central found itself ranked No. 1 in the nation by USA Today newspaper. It was both an honor and a huge distraction heading into its state quarterfinal against LaGrange and its elusive quarterback, Vince Sutton.

"We had reporters from newspapers and TV stations in hallways and the lunchroom all week," said Henderson.

Sometimes, though, there is no failure like success.

LaGrange jumped to a 28-0 lead in the first half, and Clarke never recovered. The Gladiators scored three touchdowns in the second half, and were driving for a score late in the game before time ran out. But it was too little, too late.

Clarke began what would be the first of three straight trips to the state championship game in 1984. The Gladiators, behind quarterback Chris Morocco, took a 13-1 record into the title game against Valdosta, where they lost to the Wildcats 21-14.

The 1985 team proved to be another high-scoring team, averaging 32.2 points per game. The Gladiators marched to a 15-0 record, beating Warner Robins 21-14 in the title game. Among the leaders on that team were tailback Kenny Brown, quarterback Robbie Kamerschen, who signed with Stanford, fullback David Perno, who went on to become Georgia's head baseball coach, tight end Derek Dooley, son of former Georgia head coach and athletic director Vince Dooley, and John Kasay, who set numerous Georgia kicking records and is now in the NFL with the Carolina Panthers.

"We had 10 seniors on offense," said Perno. "There were guys who had been holding hands in that huddle for five years, ever since we were on 'C' team together. We believed in the system. And we believed in Coach Henderson."

It was Clarke's third state championship in nine years. Was it the makings of a dynasty?

In 1986, Clarke took a 14-0 record and a 29-game winning streak into the championship game against Valdosta. Led by an explosive quarterback named Adrian Jarrell, who later signed with Notre Dame, the Gladiators were poised to hang another state championship banner at Death Valley.

But the Wildcats overwhelmed them, denying them the title again, as they had in 1984. Valdosta won 28-0, shutting out a team that had shut out six opponents itself during the season.

"Losing that game like we did was like a dagger in the heart," Henderson said.

The two following rebuilding seasons both produced 7-4 marks. But there were plenty of victories off the field.

"There was unity," said Wesley Middlebrooks, who played on those teams. "Blacks would spend the night with whites. Every single person on the team was treated the same way. He expected the same out of everyone. He really transformed this city. He was the glue that held it all together. He was not only respected by his own athletes but players on the other team would come up and want to shake his hand."

The 1987 team was led by defensive end Chuck Smith, who later starred at Tennessee and was a first-round draft pick of the NFL's Atlanta Falcons.

The 1989 season was one of the most unusual in Henderson's coaching career. The Gladiators opened the season with three straight losses to Cedar Shoals, R.E. Lee of Montgomery, Ala., and Statesboro.

Following the loss to Statesboro, Henderson had his players running on the track after a Sunday afternoon team meeting.

"A group of young adults was playing touch football in the stadium," Henderson recalled. "They were making a lot of noise. I asked them to be quieter but they kept getting louder so I asked them to leave.

"They reluctantly went up the stadium steps. Then, one got to the top, turned around and hollered: 'You're an old, senile Tom Landry!!!'

"I had to laugh. They were calling me an old man back in 1973."

The "old man" still knew how to coach, too.

The loss to Cedar Shoals was counted as a win, 1-0, when Cedar Shoals was found to have an ineligible player and had to forfeit.

Then the Gladiators reeled off 11 straight wins before another state championship bout with Valdosta. Once again, the Wildcats proved to be their nemesis, winning 33-13.

The same held true to form in 1990, when an 11-win season ended with an 8-0 loss to Valdosta in the state semifinals.

The Gladiators reached the quarterfinals in 1991, their third straight season with double-digit wins.

That was followed by a 12-win season in 1992, including three wins by a total of nine points in the playoffs. It set up a rematch with Valdosta in the state finals.

In the 15 seasons since Clarke had topped the Wildcats for the state crown in 1977, Valdosta had won four straight against Clarke in the playoffs.

It was a season that had seen Henderson win his 200th career game as the Gladiators coach. This time against Valdosta would prove to be no different. It also turned out to be one of the most controversial endings in Henderson's storied career.

Behind 17-14 late in the game, which was played in Valdosta, the Gladiators marched from their own 15-yard line to the Valdosta 15 on an 11-play drive. Of course, Henderson wanted to score a touchdown.

"But I also knew if we kicked a field goal, we would be co-champions," he said.

He had tremendous confidence in kicker Matt McNeil. With 2:28 left, he had McNeil line up for a 32-yard attempt.

McNeil missed the field goal.

Or did he?

"I couldn't really see from my angle," Henderson said. "But people in the end zone had their hands up."

Later, photographs enlarged from footage shot by a local television station made it appear the kick was indeed good, clearing the inside left crossbar by several feet.

"It would be several years before I could even look at the film," said Henderson. "My youngest daughter, Chris, took it hard. She couldn't understand why I didn't protest the game. But I believe if the umpire says it's a strike, it's a strike."

It would be the last time Henderson ever faced Valdosta.

The next season proved to be disastrous. The Gladiators finished 2-8, the program's first losing season since 1973, Henderson's first year at Clarke Central. It also ended a string of 18 straight playoff appearances.

One of the losses of the '93 season was a 49-0 defeat at the hands of South Gwinnett. It was the worst loss of Henderson's career. And it came against a program Henderson's team had thrashed 70-0 just 10 years earlier. So, the most lopsided victory and defeat of Henderson's coaching career came against South Gwinnett.

Naturally, questions came up about Henderson's retirement. He had turned 65 in June, that magical age to retire in some lines of work.

"Retire? People ask me that all the time," Henderson said at the time. "And when the janitor at the school starts asking me, I begin to wonder. But the fire still burns inside me the same way it always has. I'm really younger now than I was when I was 22.

"There will never be an easy time to stop coaching. I just don't want anybody having to suggest it. I don't want to be like an old fighter who goes one round too long and one fight too many."

Clarke rebounded in 1994 with a 6-4 record, but missed the playoffs again. The 1995 team went 11-2, returning to the playoffs. The season ended in the quarterfinals against Southwest DeKalb and its all-world quarterback, Quincy Carter, who went on to star at Georgia and start in the NFL for the Dallas Cowboys.

"He was one of the finest athletes I've ever seen on a high school football field," Henderson said. "He was a man among boys. I heard all the great college coaches – Bear Bryant, Joe Paterno and Woody Hayes – always say the worst thing you can try to do is coach a great athlete. You just leave him alone. When we had our great kicker, John Kasay, the only thing I ever said to him was: 'John, look how wide those goalposts are!'"

The Gladiators lost the game, 44-21. When Henderson walked off the field on that cold, December night, he had no idea it would be the last high school football game he would ever coach.

Henderson reflects beneath one of his favorite trees, overlooking the Atlantic Ocean at Jekyll Island. (Photo courtesy of Henderson family.)

IT CAN BE DONE

His daughter, Carol, had been after him to have his hearing checked. She would tell him something, and he would have to ask her to speak louder.

"Daddy," she said, "Go get a hearing test."

One afternoon, he was driving alone down Prince Avenue and he could almost hear her repeating it.

"Daddy, go get a hearing test."

He turned onto Chase Street and stopped at Dr. Phil Sheffield's office to make an appointment. Sheffield already was aware of Henderson's hearing difficulties. He didn't waste any time. He saw him right away. After checking Henderson's hearing, he immediately scheduled an MRI.

The news was not good. It was not a hearing loss brought about by old age. Henderson had a benign tumor behind his left ear resting against the base of the brain.

Spring practice was in May. By June 2, Henderson's 68th birthday, he was in a Nashville, Tenn., hospital awaiting surgery. The operation was successful, but it left him with a permanent loss of hearing in his left ear.

He asked the doctor when he could resume coaching.

"Whenever you feel like it," said the doctor.

Trouble was, he didn't feel like it. He had other issues besides just a hearing loss. It was a condition known as acoustic neuroma. The nerve damage in his inner ear left him to contend with bouts of vertigo and problems with his equilibrium. Standing and walking were difficult. He couldn't close his left eye. His lip was drooping. It would be three months before he could drive a car again.

"I had gone into that operation thinking it was going to be a piece of cake," he said. "What I failed to realize was that they had cut open my head!"

After the operation, he got plenty of get-well cards. Many of them were good-natured and light-hearted.

"One said my head was so hard they needed a hatchet to do the operation," said Henderson. "Another said when they finally got through my ear and inside my head there wasn't anything inside. One said it didn't matter that I had lost my hearing in my left ear. I never listened to anybody anyway."

All kidding aside, he began to wonder how much it would impact his ability to coach in the weeks before the start of the 1996 season.

So he went to the place where he had gone so many times for rest, relaxation and soul-searching – in the shade of the large oak trees of Jekyll Island. He spent hours sitting, reflecting and praying as he looked out into the ocean.

Then he called his entire family together and made perhaps the most difficult decision of his life.

There were enough tears to fill another ocean.

He called the school's secretary, Connie Wegmann, and asked her to type a letter of resignation to all the players and to the school's new principal, Robert Poole.

It was a pain worse than any surgery.

When he got back to Athens, he had family members go to Clarke Central to clean out his office. It hurt for him to go near the school.

"It left a real void in my life," he said. "It wasn't just coaching the players and preparing for the games. It was being at that school every day and walking those halls."

He said he felt like he "died inside." He felt as if he had let his players down.

"It was almost like guilt," he said. "I had always taught kids to never quit, to never give up."

His son-in-law Steve Brooks, was named as his successor. Carol's husband had been a loyal assistant and defensive coordinator. Henderson knew he was leaving the program in good hands.

At midseason, on Oct. 11, 1996, Clarke Central's "Death Valley Stadium" was renamed "Billy Henderson Stadium." It was written in red and gold letters on top of the press box.

Henderson's favorite saying, "It Can Be Done," was etched on a granite marker bearing his likeness behind the home bleachers.

"Anything that has happened tonight is a direct reflection of the love affair I have with this school and this community," Henderson told the crowd.

The stadium ceremony was an emotional night for Henderson, but it was not without its share of humor. Before the marker was unveiled, Lamar Thaxton, a local high school official, threw a flag at Henderson's feet. He presented Henderson with a silver tray and made him an "honorary official" because "he always made the calls anyway."

Never one with idle hands, it was just a matter of time before

Henderson's health improved, and he began to involve himself in other things. In December 1996, he joined the staff of the YMCA as director of the youth football programs. He had been alarmed at the decline in participation.

"I drove by the field one day and saw how the numbers had gone down," he said.

So he joined one of his former Athens High players, YMCA executive director John Simpson, and was given the responsibilities of overseeing the league, creating interest and conducting youth football camps.

Henderson used the same successful approach he had used to generate interest in his high school programs. He went around to all the elementary schools, gave pep talks and showed promotional films about football. By the next year, enrollment had tripled.

Henderson was so excited to be working around young players in the Y's football program he would often wait on the bench for them to get off the bus from school.

There was also a time in early 1998 when Henderson believed he might be fully recovered enough to return to coaching. Although half his hearing was gone, and his step had slowed, there was still a fire in his belly.

He admitted he was restless, like an injured player who wants to get back in the game. He missed the sidelines, the rhythm of the seasons, the associations with the players, students, coaches, faculty and fans.

In a span of five days, Henderson pursued the head football coaching position at Central-Macon, accepted the job, then reconsidered his decision and turned it down.

Central principal Steve Smith, now school superintendent of Lowndes County in Valdosta, was a Willingham graduate and broke into coaching as a member of one of Henderson's first staffs at Clarke Central.

Smith had introduced Henderson as the new coach the previous week, fielding questions about Henderson's age (69) and health. The school board unanimously approved hiring him on Jan. 29, 1998.

But Henderson began to have second thoughts shortly after taking the reins of Central, the school that had been created from his alma mater, Lanier.

"I felt like the little boy up on the high dive with his stomach churning," he told one sports writer.

His decision to withdraw his name came after he had driven to St. Augustine, Fla., to attend the wedding of a friend, Daniel Veal.

Crossing a bridge in Jacksonville, Henderson said a strange

feeling swept over him. All he could think about was Athens. Home. Friends. Family.

Ultimately, Henderson realized he "couldn't give it my all."

Walking away again was just as difficult. He had been getting ready to paint the Central gym. He had ordered equipment for the weight room. He had started meeting with parents and players.

Henderson said he realized he had been obsessed to coach again. Now he had total peace about his decision to stay retired.

It was Feb. 2, Groundhog's Day. No shadows. He could retire emotionally from coaching the game he loved.

"Reversing my field is a hard thing to do," he said. "But there's no question it was the right thing to do. ... The most significant part of my visit was the interview I had with the board of education. These men and women asked some hard and honest questions that needed to be asked and had to do with concerns that I had not given a thought: Why does a person who is 69 years of age consider coaching?'"

Those closest to Henderson knew retirement would not stop him. It would barely slow him down.

He continued to be involved in numerous projects, including the Champions Foundation and the Athens Athletic Hall of Fame. He also has remained religious about his daily exercise routine at the YMCA.

He remained a loyal friend to everyone who ever crossed his path. Two who stayed very close were civic leader Claude Williams and the late Harold Huff, who was a former player under Henderson at Athens High and became chaplain of the Clarke Central team in 1982.

The beginnings of the Champions Foundation actually had its roots in 1951 when Henderson was at Jefferson. Henderson and others were able to utilize school facilities and local coaches to operate summer programs for children and youth in the community.

He had tried to sell the idea to city leaders in Macon in the early 1960s, but it fell on deaf ears. Finally, a city official named Agnes Hatcher was the only one who would listen. (Her son, Edgar, became a head football coach in Macon. Her grandson, Chris, is currently the head coach at Valdosta State.)

She liked the idea and convinced the city to appropriate funds. Henderson introduced the Champions Foundation in Athens in the 1970s. Its mission statement is "to expose people to positive environments that promote spiritual values, patriotism, physical fitness, desirable habits and skills in sports and the desire to excel in all endeavors."

The Champions Foundation continues to receive the support of Athens business and community leaders. Its goal is to provide summer day camps and specialized sports camps, support youth and high school football, help high school students find athletic scholarships and promote sportsmanship at schools, civic clubs and churches.

Henderson also founded the Athens Athletic Hall of Fame in 2000. He organized community leaders and started a foundation with an annual budget of about $40,000.

And he recruited folks like Oby Dupree to serve with him as a charter member on the board of directors.

"I didn't know that much about athletics," she said. "What caught my eye was Billy Henderson and the way he handled himself. Here is a man who wakes up every day of his life asking not what he can do for himself but what he can do for others."

She had always been impressed with Henderson because of the way he treated her daughter, Betsy, when she was a student at Clarke Central. "She wasn't a cheerleader, and she didn't date a football player," said Dupree. "But he always took time with her. She once told me he was the sweetest, finest, caring man she had ever known. Here was this rugged, rough man talking to her about God! It really touched me what he had done for her."

The hall of fame's first inductee was an African-American, Pleas "Clegg" Starks, a longtime waterboy for the University of Georgia.

Henderson remains one of the most recognizable names, faces and crew cuts in a town that is full of sports heroes.

His final record at Clarke Central was 222-65-1, and his overall coaching record was 286-107-15, making him one of the winningest coaches in Georgia high school history. At Clarke, his teams reached the playoffs 18 straight years.

As a head coach, he won three state championships in football, three in baseball and one in swimming.

At Clarke Central, more than 160 young men received college football scholarships.

"You hear about the ones who go to Georgia, Alabama, Notre Dame and Clemson," said veteran sports writer Billy Harper. "What a lot of people don't realize is all those other young men who have a chance to get a college education playing at schools like Western Carolina and

Appalachian State, all because of Coach Henderson."

Those who have been around him also realize that for every Billy Henderson story you see, hear or read, there are dozens that go untold.

Like the time he paid the overdue bills of one of his players who had the electricity cut off in his family's home. Or the time he loaned his car to a player from a divorced family so the young man could visit his father in Atlanta on Thanksgiving Day.

"He has always loved everybody the same," said his daughter, Fran. "I remember he had to get one of his football players out of jail, and he came to live with us. There were others he opened our home to until they were able to get on their feet. One of them even taught me to drive. Daddy would give them money when he sometimes didn't even have enough to put clothes on the backs of his own family."

There are burdens he must carry, too.

He continues to be a caregiver for Fosky, who suffers from dementia. The days and nights are grueling as he watches her health slip and watches her struggle with a disease that is often known as the "long good-bye."

He has a grandson, Craig, who is Steve and Carol's son. Craig was born with several congenital birth defects, including an incomplete esophagus and eyes which did not develop. He did not come home from the hospital until he was 3 months old. He has never spoken.

"They said his life expectancy was about 7 years," said Henderson. "He's now 19 years old. Carol, Steve and Craig's sisters, Stefanie and Sarah, all take care of him. The whole family is a profile in courage. Love is sustaining."

Henderson has another grandson, Zach, who belongs to son Johnny and is expected to battle for the starting quarterback job at Clarke Central in the fall of 2005.

Like his dad, Johnny Henderson became a coach on the staffs at North Carolina State and the University of Tennessee at Chattanooga. He now works at a car dealership in Athens.

Johnny and his wife, Pat, have an older son, Bradford, who is a computer science major at Gainesville Junior College in Athens.

Fran and her husband, Jim Hobbs, have two children. Daughter Jenny is studying hotel management in Denver, Colo. Kim is majoring in journalism at Samford University in Birmingham.

Carol and her husband, Steve Brooks, have three children. Craig is the middle child. Daughter Stefanie is in nursing school at Mercer University in Atlanta. Sarah is a seventh-grade student at St. Joseph School in Athens.

Chris and her husband, Perry, have two sons. Matthew is majoring in French at Kennesaw State University. Zachary is in the sixth grade at Durham Middle School in Kennesaw.

Henderson's players still call him. They are still involved in his life. He is still involved in their lives, too.

A former player, Tate Grizzle, recently contacted him. He said he wanted to thank Henderson for teaching him to have a firm handshake and to always look people in the eye when he talked to them.

"Next to my parents, he has been the most influential person in my life," Grizzle said.

"I still call him when I'm in Athens, and we get together at The Varsity for a chili dog," said Marvin Hall, who was on his first high school squad at Jefferson in 1951.

And Henderson never fails to stop teaching and coaching, whenever the opportunity presents itself.

On a recent summer morning, he was going for a swim at the YMCA. As he was getting into the pool, he asked a group of young boys if they wanted to race.

One boy looked up at Henderson and told him he didn't know how to swim.

"Well," said the coach, "you're about to learn."

"It was a beautiful thing to watch him gradually gain confidence," said Henderson. "When I left, he was still out there practicing. I was so overjoyed. It was like I had hit a home run."

He leaves his mark in other ways.

On another recent summer day, he was walking in the neighborhood and it began to rain. Suddenly, the rain became a downpour, and Henderson was getting drenched.

A woman in a truck saw him, stopped and rolled down her window.

"What are you doing, Coach?"

He recognized her as a former student at Clarke Central. He didn't remember her name, or what year she graduated, just that she was there. That her blood ran red and gold. And that she smiled.

"Don't you remember what I used to tell you at Clarke Central," he said. "It never rains on Gladiators."

No, in fact, the sun seems to shine wherever Billy Henderson goes. It was shining at Athens Regional Hospital this past December, when he got a call from Madeline Van Dyck, a former school nurse at Clarke Central who was supervisor of student nurses at the hospital.

She told him she had a patient who was gravely ill and suffering from a bout of depression. Then she mentioned his name, Hamp Tanner. He had been a teammate of Henderson's at both Lanier and Georgia.

So Henderson visited Tanner in the hospital. They swapped stories about their playing days. The smile returned to Tanner's face.

By the next time he visited, Henderson had arranged to have films of Georgia games with Auburn and Georgia Tech in 1947 and North Carolina in 1948. Steve Colquitt, editor of "Bulldog Magazine," arranged to get him the vintage films.

"We relived some of our happiest moments," he said.

Two days later, Tanner died.

His impact has known no boundaries – former teammates, students, team managers, cheerleaders, coaches and sports writers.

"I think he was one of the greatest motivators in the history of coaching at any level," said the late Harley Bowers, a longtime sports columnist for "The Macon Telegraph." "He could take players and get the most out of them as well as anybody I've ever seen. You can't say this about many people, but he was the kind of coach that no matter where he was, he would be a winner."

There are people like Jimmy Hammond, who doesn't know where he would be today had Henderson not been a part of his life. Hammond went on to become a high school coach himself at a now-defunct school known as Southeast-Macon.

Hammond was a troubled teenager, saw upheaval in his family life, and ran with the wrong crowd. Then, on a summer's night in 1958, his life changed at the old Dairy Queen on Houston Avenue.

"There was this guy standing at the window with a flat top, white shirt and little bitty tie," said Hammond. "I had never seen him before in my life. But he came up, shook my hand and introduced himself. He asked me how much I weighed, and I told him 142 pounds. He told me I was a nice-sized kid, and that he was taking the football team to Jekyll Island the next day. He asked me to meet them at the school at 8 o'clock in the morning. I went home and put my clothes in a sack because I didn't have a suitcase.

"He cared enough about me to make a difference in my life, and I've never forgotten it."

There also have been folks like Carl Summers, a former Willingham player and assistant coach, who credits the "never give up" ethic Henderson instilled in him with saving his life when he was wounded in Vietnam.

There have been the Eddie Battles, too. Battle was Henderson's first quarterback at Willingham, and the first athlete from the Macon school to earn a college scholarship. He still calls and visits Henderson on a regular basis.

Although Henderson lives in Athens and Battle is in Macon, it is almost a father-son relationship.

And there are people like Charles Belflower, who became the statistician and sports information director at Clarke Central. Henderson inspired him and gave him a purpose in life at a time he needed it most.

"He has had an impact on so many lives," said his daughter, Fran. "He helped young boys believe in themselves. He was drawn to young men from single-parent homes because he was from a situation just like that. He's just a strong force, teaching them they are just like anybody else. He made them belong. And they believe in themselves. You can't get any more powerful than that."

It Can Be Done.

TESTIMONIALS

There is no question that anything I have ever accomplished in my life has been because of the grace of God and my association with Billy Henderson.

As a student at Clarke Central High School, I was sitting in the gym for a football pep rally on Dec. 7, 1979. It was the day before Clarke Central would defeat Tift County for Billy Henderson's second state football title.

Billy came to the middle of the gym floor that day to speak to the crowd of more than 1,500 students. Billy commanded such respect from the student body that you could have heard a pin drop when he took the microphone.

Billy never spoke about the upcoming game during that three-minute speech. Rather he talked about students who had no plan in life and maybe were involved in destructive forces like drugs and alcohol. He challenged the crowd that day to get involved in wholesome activities, such as sports. He mentioned the fact that he jogged down Milledge Avenue daily.

God spoke one day and said, "Billy, try harder. Try harder."

God spoke to me, too. His message came to me through Billy Henderson on that December day. Little did I know that, by heeding the call to get involved with Clarke Central football, I would lead a wonderful life. Later, I would have opportunities in athletics at the University of Georgia, Oklahoma and Georgia Southern University. I would also have a chance to work in broadcasting and politics.

Having served as Billy Henderson's unofficial press agent and biographer for more than 25 years, I have assisted several would-be authors in their attempts to write books about him. None have ever been published. I have attempted this myself several times, but I finally settled for producing a 90-minute video on Billy's life in 1993.

It is only fitting that the man who finally got the job done is from Macon, Ga., a place where Billy first rose to national prominence as a high school athlete at Lanier High and later coached for 15 years at Willingham High and Mount de Sales.

Well-known "Macon Telegraph" columnist Ed Grisamore paints a portrait of Billy not generally known by the public. Ed fills in the details as he recounts stories from the time Billy was born in Dublin, Ga., through 45 years of coaching to his current position as executive director of the Athens Athletic Hall of Fame.

Ed covers it all – the triumphs, the tragedies, the wins, the losses, and interviews many of the people Billy has touched during his lifetime. We see Billy as a fire-breathing taskmaster on the field but also one who would be ready to help anyone in need at a moment's notice. This is a book that will serve as a reminder to everyone today and for generations to come that IT CAN BE DONE." — *Charles Belflower. Clark Central football historian.*

"In my 30 years of covering sports, I never met a more impressive coach, including those on the college level." — *Billy Harper. Former Athens Banner-Herald sport writer.*

"Where can I start? How do I comment on someone who, in five short years of my high school experience affects what and how I do everything every day? I have been incredibly blessed by God in my family and business.

One of the ways Coach Henderson prepared me to hang tough and never quit was on a hot, humid, yet dry piece of dirt out on Canterbury Road in South Macon.

After experiencing five years of football practices there, where lessons in survival as a lineman in practice were far more important than those learned on Friday night, the challenges of the business world have seemed rather mundane. Learning to quickly count who I was matched with in the line for tackling drills, when I was the runner, has served me greatly in learning the importance of understanding numbers at a glance. Learning how to negotiate with those who had not counted so well so they would be tackled by Wayne Spence or Gene Crump taught me quick negotiating skills.

And learning how to run 'hats' until I dropped has taught me that the end will come, just don't quit and you will win. I also learned to respect everyone, and understand the importance of everyone, regardless of their station in life.

When my wife and I had a chance to be in the White House for the Christmas party with President Bush and his wife, Laura, the last thing I did before going was to call Coach Henderson and thank him for getting me there. His impact on me cannot be overstated. It is there in the fiber of my being, and I do thank God that he gave me those glorious, hard, and growing days with Coach Billy Henderson." — *Ben Hinson. Former Willingham athlete. President, Mid Georgia Ambulance, Macon.*

"I moved to Athens the summer before my junior year of high school in 1989. I spent that summer working out and practicing with the Gladiators. Although things did not work out for me at Clarke Central, the relationship that was built with Coach Henderson during those four months has had a profound effect on my life. I have kept correspondence with Billy at least twice a year since 1991, and every time I talk with him he inspires me to be a better man.

I remember the first day I met him. He took me aside and told me he was raised without a father, just as I was, and how it is important to take care of your mother and be a good person. He told me about how he would arrive at the school at 5 a.m. to run, and as he finished in the parking lot he would take an extra lap, closing his eyes and imagining an arena full of cheering fans as he carried the Olympic torch.

One time, he asked me if I wanted to see a quarterback play the game as it is meant to be played. It was old reels of Brad, his son, at age 16 playing in black and white. He was right. Brad was amazing. There is the time he took me to the Varsity for a chili dog, and the entire place got quiet as people stared at him the way people stare at greatness.

Billy Henderson is the greatest man I have been fortunate enough to know. I spent four months under his tutelage as a young man, and 14 years of correspondence. Not once have we ever had an idle chat. He is always teaching, always giving of himself. He is a true Christian, and I am better for having known him.

Last year, I was having the dilemma many coaches face. Income is not the strength of an early coaching career, and I was doubting my chosen profession. I had not talked to Coach Henderson in almost a year, when one night I came home to a message on my answering machine: "Dusty, this is Billy Henderson. I was thinking of you and wanted to call. I remember when I was a young coach with a family. Money was tight. Stay strong." It was just what I needed to get me through. How did he know?

I'm thankful he is my mentor and blessed he is my friend. I believe him to be one of this country's finest sons." — *Dusty M. Gunn. Former Cedar Shoals quarterback, now a high school coach in Maryland.*

"Billy has done more for the youth of the Athens community than any other man I know. Not only from the activities he provides and sponsors, but also from the example he sets in his unique style of motivation. His leadership does not end with our youth. His enthusiasm for life, his positive attitude, high standards, and emphasis on how you play the game provide a road map to success for any business." — *Lewis Shropshire. President, Motel Enterprises, Inc., Athens*

"Billy Henderson is one of the finest Georgians and Americans I have ever known. He was a great high school athlete at Lanier High in Macon when I was prep editor of The Atlanta Journal right after World War II. He was an outstanding baseball and football player at the University of Georgia when I was sports information director. I nicknamed him the 'Macon Meteor' for his blazing speed afoot. At Clarke Central High School in Athens, his football coaching success was fabulous. And he is still rendering superb civic services as founder and promoter of the Athens Athletic Hall of Fame." — *Dan Magill. Legendary UGA tennis coach.*

"The first thing I remember about Billy Henderson was his celebrated speed in the Ogeechee League. He played in my hometown of Wrightsville, and I remember the old-timers talking about how fast he was on the base paths.

Through the years, I crossed paths with him often as a successful high school coach. Finishing his career at Clarke Central, there was an opportunity to see his teams play frequently. And I always appreciated that he was a sound, fundamental coach like his old college coach — Wallace Butts.

Often, when I would ride down Milledge Avenue, I would see him jogging, trim and fit, accompanied by his ever-present crew cut. What did that crew cut mean? Probably that he was a traditionalist, and that when he made a change as a coach, it was for the better but had to make sound fundamental sense.

No coach with his experience would fail to remind you that football is a game of blocking and tackling. You get away from that emphasis, you are not going to succeed. Billy succeeded because of adherence to fundamentals.

He was always paying tribute to his teams and players. If a player achieved something on the field and beyond, Bill was always congratulating him and finding a way for him to come home to be recognized. Tribute by the home folks. That is the greatest tribute of all." — *Loran Smith. UGA football broadcaster.*

"We were kids from blue-collar homes, the sons of World War II veterans who were settling in those South Macon neighborhoods. Coach Henderson had this ability to make you believe in yourself. People played above their ability. He would tell you to run through a brick wall, and you would say to yourself, 'OK, I will.' He would tell you the other team put on their pants one leg at a time, just like you do. That helped me in the business world. I have never been intimidated by the competition." — *Wayne Johnson. Captain, 1964 Willingham Rams. Offensive lineman, Florida State.*

"Coach Henderson changed the direction of my life in the seventh grade. Because of him, I knew I wanted to follow his lead and become a coach. The most impressive thing about him was his level of confidence, the way he carried himself. He was never arrogant. He never crossed the line. He always has had the kind of energy that is inspiring." — *David Perno. Member Clarke Central 1985 state championship team. Head Baseball Coach, University of Georgia.*

"He was a great all-around athlete, terrific coach and family man. His players loved him, and I can truly say he put his players first. He played by the rules and had deep faith in what the Good Man expected of him.

The nicest compliment is I would have been happy for my son, Bucky, to have played for him." — *Howard "Doc" Ayers. Former UGA Coach*

"He always had a knack for making everybody feel important. It didn't matter how good or bad a player you were, whether you played an instrument in the band, were just a regular student, a cheerleader or a majorette. He made everybody feel as important as if they were the starting quarterback." — *Eddie Battle, Willingham's first quarterback in 1958.*

"I have known Billy since we were teammates in baseball at Georgia from 1948-50. I can honestly say he is one of the most dedicated people I know. He is respected and admired by his former players and coaches and will leave a huge legacy. He deserves all the accolades he receives, and I'm proud to call him friend." — *Roland "Hank" Condon. Former UGA baseball teammate.*

"I remember when Don Hight, principal of Clarke Central, came to me and said, 'We are looking for a new coach. Who would you get?'

I told him without hesitation that my No. 1 choice would be Coach Billy Henderson from Macon. I was so impressed by him when I played football and baseball against his Willingham teams.

The rest is history. What a great job he did at Clarke Central and what a great influence he has had on the youth and community of Athens. We have been blessed to have him as a coach, contributor, and, most of all, a friend." — *Woody Chastain. Owner, Bulldog Sporting Goods, Athens.*

"We went to high school together and, even though we came from different backgrounds, we remain friends to this day because of our value system. That's what being friends is all about. We celebrated our differences.

Billy is a multi-faceted man. He is a salesman, a preacher, a patriot, a family man and a coach. And he is a loyal friend. If you know Billy Henderson, you know he is always there for you. I'm proud to be part of his life." — *Melvin Kruger, CEO, L.E. Schwartz & Son, Macon.*

"I had the pleasure of playing for Coach Henderson on his first two teams at Clarke Central. I have never met a more positive, enthusiastic and energetic individual. While Coach Henderson could have been successful in any profession, he chose to spend his life teaching young people. What a blessing he has been to the Athens community for the past 32 years!" — *Tim Mackey, 1973 Clarke Central team, Athens businessman.*

"Mental toughness. I learned that from Coach Henderson. It has helped me succeed not only in my future athletic opportunities, but more importantly helps me to this day succeed in the game of life."— *Jim Bob Harris. Quarterback, 1977 Clarke Central state championship team.*

"In 1958, Coach Billy Henderson appeared on the South Macon scene, and that working-class side of town has never been the same. He created pride, tradition, and an identity in an area of Macon that previously had none. His teams were always tough, competitive, well-prepared, and were winners as they mirrored the character of their coach. Lots of coaches know X's and O's; Coach Henderson knew young men. He wrote the book on how to get inside the hearts, souls, and minds of young men. He could get more effort and results from teenage athletes than they knew they were capable of giving.

He was born to coach, and in my opinion, the greatest coaches of all time aren't measured by won/lost percentages. They are measured by the numbers of lives that have been influenced and enriched.

You see, those are the types of guys I have always wanted my son to be influenced by, just as I was influenced by the best." — *Joe McDaniel. Former Willingham player and Mount de Sales coach. Now ordained minister, director of public information for Mid Georgia Ambulance and author of the book, "31206: The Boys of Willingham High."*

"Coach Henderson had a burning desire to see young people succeed. Whether they were in the athletic arena, in the classroom, on the cheerleading squad, or in the drama club, he believed in success. On a hot August day, during a tough football practice, he had an innate ability to reach us when we were at our absolute worst, break us down, and force us to look deep inside ourselves to discover our true potential. His trophy room is full of those who followed his plan for success: college and pro-athletes, lawyers, doctors, entrepreneurs, ministers, and businessmen. His legacy continues to live on in Macon today, as his ideals of success have been the inspiration for the Macon Sports Hall of Fame Youth Camp and Macon Youth Day. He is truly an inspiration to all who played for him and to all that know him." — *Phil McGoldrick, former Mount de Sales player. Now with Snow's Memorial Chapel, Macon.*

"Being a long-time Athens resident and Bulldog fan, I first knew Billy Henderson as an outstanding football and baseball player for the University of Georgia. Following his return to Athens in 1973 as head coach at Clarke Central, I've come to know Billy quite well.

One of the many highlights of our 33-year friendship came in June 2004 when I was privileged to join with the Henderson family in Dalton for his induction into the Georgia Athletic Coaches Hall of Fame.

Don Hight, former principal at Clarke Central and the man who brought Billy back to Athens, said the following in his introduction: "The impact Coach Henderson had on high school sports in our state during his 42-year high school coaching career is unsurpassed. His passion for sports, for education, for understanding, and for civic-mindedness are matched only by his deep faith. Although now retired, he continues to work for the same things that have been his mainstay throughout his coaching career as he tirelessly works for the Champions Foundation, an organization he established more than 20 years ago. He devoted his life to enriching young people through high school sports and will long be remembered for his sensational career." Amen and amen! – *Claude Williams, Athens civic leader.*

"It has been my privilege to serve as his pastor for more than 24 years. I knew him in the height of his coaching success, and I have the opportunity to see him now as a devoted husband caring for Fosky with the physical challenges she has. He is tender and helpful to her.

Billy gave me and some musicians from our church the opportunity to conduct a voluntary service for the football team each year before they left for summer camp at Jekyll Island. The blessings from that continue to this day as parents will say, "I loved those services, they were so helpful to my son."

Billy did a great job teaching character to his players as well as football skills. That was the first thing I ever heard about him, and then seeing him up close and personal I found it to be true.

He once told me that one of the things of which he was most proud in his life was that, at Clarke Central at least, he did not cut anyone. If they stuck it out through practice they would be on the team. Who knows how much that contributed to the self-esteem of kids who might not have had a lot of athletic ability but had endurance. That is a great contribution to make to a kid's development." – *Stewart Simms, Jr. Pastor, Beech Haven Baptist Church, Athens.*

"Billy Henderson is without a doubt one of the most interesting men that I have had the pleasure of getting to know. I first came to know Coach Henderson when I was in his P. E. classes after transferring to Willingham in 1960. Even as a teenager, I realized what talents he possessed and what a motivator he was. At pep rallies he had a way of making the hair stand up on your neck as he talked about the school and the love he had for it. He made us believe that the Willingham Rams were No. 1 and that whomever we were playing on Friday nights belonged to us. He made us particularly proud when we had the fortune of beating Lanier at Porter Stadium in front of standing room only crowds, in what was the greatest high school rivalry that Macon has ever known.

Billy also has an unusual knack for great storytelling. I had the privilege of interviewing him three times between 1996 and 1998 for a television program I hosted in Macon called Keeping In Touch. My life has been enhanced by havi' the opportunity not only to be a student of Coach Henderson's but by getting to know him later in life. He has had a more positive influence on young people's lives during his lifetime than most men. With characteristic humility, however, Billy always credits these accomplishments to the profound influence of his God-fearing and self-sacrificing mother. I think his character and perseverance had a little to do with it, too." – *Aubrey Hammack, 1963 graduate of Willingham High School.*

"He is one of the best friends I've ever had, and we are still very close. He has always cared about people, and he lets you know he cares about you. He's not afraid to hide it. I think he's one of the greatest motivators to ever live. People say he would have been a millionaire if he had been a salesman. Well, he has sold people on being the best they could be." – *Edgar Hatcher, longtime Macon football coach and father of Valdosta State Head Coach Chris Hatcher.*

"When I first moved to Athens, Billy and I were neighbors, living on the same street 10 houses apart. He saw my 6-year-old son, Anton, and I out front playing catch. The next day, he came by with football pads, a helmet and a time when Anton was to report to the YMCA for practice. Billy didn't know it at the time, but we couldn't afford for Anton to play. He was able to play the end of that season and enjoy the thrill of suiting up at Sanford Stadium prior to the Georgia-Georgia Tech game.

One image I have of Billy Henderson came when I had a personal crisis in my life. The engine had just blown up on our car. We had gone without two cars as a family for nearly two years after our van had been totaled in an accident. We purchased a used car, and it lasted a year. The next day, Billy drove up with a Chevy Malibu, handed me the keys and was getting read to walk back to his house. It was his car he leased for his wife, Fosky, who was no longer able to drive. The gesture brought tears to us. His kindness, compassion and desire to meet a need for anyone, anywhere shows no boundaries.

My third image of Coach Henderson came during my reporting on "Heaven and Hell" – the Jekyll Island football camp and its history since Billy began coaching at Clarke Central. He brought together rich and poor, black and white in a way similar to the "Remember the Titans" movie. What he did for those kids – teaching them passion, discipline, work ethic and a love for Jesus Christ – and how grown men talked about it 20 years later, you cannot describe. Thousands of lives were forever altered for the good because of their chance encounter for a brief period with the man they know just as Coach Henderson." – *Brad Zimanek, former sports editor, Athens Banner-Herald and Daily News.*

ACKNOWLEDGEMENTS

Books do not write themselves. Coach Henderson and I would like to thank the following people for their gracious assistance and unwavering support in making this book possible.

We wish to thank Billy's family – Fosky, Carol, Fran, Johnny and Chris for their tireless contributions, and to Shirley Davenport, who watched Fosky so Billy could devote his time and energy to the book. Also to Ed's family – Delinda, Ed, Grant and Jake – who kept the home fires burning while he worked on this book, in addition to publishing another collection of columns, "Smack Dab in Dog Crossing," in March 2005.

Many thanks to Henry Beers, Gary Pulliam, Rick Hutto, Julianne Gleaton, Joni Woolf, Mary Robinson and Daniel Emerson, the remarkable staff at Indigo Publishing/Henchard Press in Macon, for having faith in "It Can Be Done." We proved that it can.

A heartfelt thanks to Lewis Shropshire and the staff at Coach Henderson's office – otherwise known as the Holiday Inn in Athens. Thanks to Charles Belflower, for being the unofficial historian and enthusiastic supporter of the book.

We want to acknowledge Athens photographers Wingate Downs, Don Nelson and Jeff Blake for the use of their photographs. Former Athens sports writer Billy Harper and his wife, Frances, also were generous with their time and talents. Special thanks to Aubrey Hammack for providing the insightful TV interviews he conducted with Coach Henderson.

Extensive background on Coach Henderson's playing and coaching career would not have been possible without reaching deep into the archives of *The Athens Banner Herald and Daily News*, *The Macon Telegraph*, *The Atlanta Journal and Constitution*, *Athens Observer*, *Athens Magazine* and *Georgia Trend* magazine.

Thanks also to Claude Felton and Christopher Lakos of the Georgia Sports Communications Department and Alan Robison and Robbie Burns of the Georgia Sports Hall of Fame.

Others who should take a bow are Dave Williams, James Holland, Joe McDaniel, Cecil Bentley, Melvin Kruger, Chris Starrs, Johnny Reynolds, Jack Davis, Demaris and Ray Turk, Oby Dupree, Judd Guest, Jon Ward, Billy Slaughter, Gene Asher, John Alexander, Wayne Dean, Jimmy Triesman, Joey Dillard, Ricky Smith, Claude Williams, Phil McGoldrick, Bill Pilcher, Robert Seay, Edgar Hatcher, Mary Beth McDonald and Gena Wages.

In 1996, Clarke Central's Stadium was renamed after Henderson.
(Photo courtesy of Jeff Blake.)

THE HENDERSON LEGACY

Willingham Football Scholarships under Henderson

1960: Eddie Battle (Newberry), Charles Partridge (Newberry).

1961: Wilton Marchman (Tennessee-Martin)

1962: Randy Wheeler (Georgia), Doug Boyd (Clemson), Jimmy Hammond (Tennessee-Martin), Joel Dickens (Tennessee-Martin).

1963: Tom Lindsey (Tennessee-Martin), Pete Gaines (Georgia), Bobby Bryant (South Carolina), Mark Bowen (Georgia).

1964: Carlie McNeil (Florida State), Terry Colson (Brigham Young), Floyd Evans (Presbyterian).

1965: Richard Whitfield (Tennessee-Martin), Carl Summers (Tennessee-Martin), Wayne Johnson (Florida State), Barney Kinard (Georgia Tech), Greg Helmuth (UT-Chattanooga), Bobby Floyd (Troy State).

1966: Derrell Parker (Georgia Tech), James Holland (Georgia Tech).

1967: Ronnie Wallace (Florida State), Durwood Sauls (Auburn), Chuck Cross (Furman).

1968: Wayne Spence (Florida State), Wayne Jones (Presbyterian), Mike Bloodworth (Newberry).

1970: Willie Goolsby (Carson-Newman).

Willingham Football Players in Pros under Henderson

1967: Bobby Bryant, (Minnesota Vikings.)

Clarke Central Senior Lettermen under Henderson

1973: Steve Bell, Lee Dennis, Brian Fosgate, Lee Gaby, Keith Griffin, Joe Mason, Clayton Mealor, Ricky Nash, Bruce Perkins, Kevin Potts, Bennie Tillman, Steve Tingle, Scott Andrews, Marion Marshall, Don Bowers, Seyborn Gordon.

1974: Tom Gary, Doug Henson, Alonzo Howard, Tim Mackey, Mike Ozburn, Andy Gibson, Ronnie Hix, Marty Escoe, Dave Hudgins, Nick Colquitt, Chuck Conley, Roger Adams, Dave Johnson, Kevin House, Tonto Norman, Jeff Ingram, Jim Hudgins.

1975: Reggie Bolton, Pat Kelley, Richard Barnett, Frank Smith, Larry

Mealor, Kenny Jackson, Homer Hector, Jeff Langford, James Davis, Mike Manley, Joe Gaines, Tony Stovall.

1976: Mike Gaines, Bob Williams, Bob McLeod, Clete Favors, Don Maxey, Elvis Schell, Quinton Bridges, Danny Riddle, Clay Carter, Glenn Guest, Jack Langford, Julian Brown, Charles Griffith, Billy Carmichael, George Kesler, Doug Evans, Ricky Smith, Chris Bizzle, John Brice, Tim Lally, Ricky Stancell.

1977: Albert Watkins, Dave Williams, Jeff Dean, Jim Bob Harris, Greg Neal, Stan Davis, Curtis Smith, Karey Johnson, Lionel Huff, Bob Weathersby, Alex Forrester, Sam Wiebe, Anthony Myrick, Jeff Turk, Ernest Eberhart, Phil Nelms, Carey Nelms, Brent Snyder, Steve Dailey, Charles Campbell, Larry Richards.

1978: :Lou Trousdale, Jerry Alexander, Richard Shiels, Reeves Carter, Eddie Lee Clarke, Craig Myers, Chris Foster, Greg Love, Randy Erwin, David Schell, Will Kelly, Hillary Billups, Mark Dailey, Danny Haynes, Johnny DeFelice, Scott Wortham, Mac McCoy, Vince Bush, Eddie Wortham, Mitch Hughes, Ken Lawrence, Mike Strickland, Todd Clark, Tony Goote, Tim Marable, Chris Bizzle, Rufus Sadler.

1979: Scott Mitchell, Blake McCrary, Mim Rice, Lee Gathreaux, Bart Richards, Ricky Green, Ron Young, Mark Long, Terry Jackson, Charley Dean, Tom Weeley, Harry Spratlin, Dwayne Harden, Dan Quillian, Jerom Sims, Walker Whitmire, Carey Colquitt, Rufus Paine David Gresham, Josh Starks, Stanley Stroud, Rufus Hope, Bubba Connell, Marcus Stephens, Ronald Brown, Joe Marshall.

1980: John Schramm, Herman Holmes, Darryl Moore, Clarence Wright, Arthur Jones, Rivington Cole, Brian Laster, Scott Strickland, Bill Falconer, Kelly Crawford, Brian Hooper, Rodney Stroud, Jay Ebert, Frank Smith, Ernie Mitchell, Fred Muckle, Bobby Lewis, James Johnson, Steve Kamerschen, Mike Tully, Roby Redwine, Percy Jordan, Frank Bush, Robert David, Bill Schubring, Chip Tardy, Damon Pope, Jim Paine, Jeff Brannon, Eric Griffith, Doug Robinson, Michael Beckner, Greg Jeffreys, Jeff McElheney, Mark Johnson, Robert Eberhart.

1981: Eric Steffe, Dean Shirley, Steve Ervin, Bobby Payne, Stanley Richardon, Mark Mitchell, Horner Asberry, David Wortham, Ricky Schell, Tracy Schell, Bruce Haygood, Gerald Mayfield, Chico Ellis, Pat Herold, Randolph Wooten, Brian Kemp, Eric Burrell, Brian Edwards, Daniel Dooley, Chuck McCrary, Bill Gauthreaux, Carlton Williams, Stuart Lay.

1982: Joel Riddle, David Bell, Alvin Jeffreys, David Dukes, Bob Tardy, Mark King, Eddy Draper, Kenny Booker, Donn Perno, Mike Cooper,

Pappy Golob, Scott Kesler, Rod Thomas, Trey Salmon, Steve Burrell, Elliott Walker, Chris Maxon, Blake Mitchell, Chris Conine, Jonathan Heyr, Greg Maye, Kevin Terrell, Henry Haynes, Terry Williams, Rickey Robinson, Greg Williams, Darrien Smith.

1983: James Barnett, John Parker, Rodney Smith, Robin Billups, Leroy Johnson, David Lester, Greg Moses, Pat Thomasson, Vic Melio, Mike Flint, Kevin Harry, Bryan Wheeler, Paul Bowles, Rick Mason, Andy Williamson, Andy Nunez, Robbie Garrison, Dan Henson, Todd Dunn, Jason Johnson, Anthony Turner, Arnold Grier, Jeff Pope Mike Hunter, Henry Williams.

1984: Daryl Brown, Maurice Brown, Doug Davenport, Tony Dunn, Amp Foster, Barry Glenn, Norbert Goodrum, Kevin Haffner, Jerry Harris, Bob Hawk, Daryl Hood, Tony Howard, Theotis King, Steve Law, Mark Lewis, Derrick Little, Chip McGinley, Todd Moody, Chris Morocco, David Nelson, Brack Rowe, Tony Seals, William Stephens, Bernard Thomas, Marvin Walker, Stan Wilbanks, Eric Wilson.

1985: Jeff Bailey, Terry Baughns, Chris Beck, Clint Bennet, Terry Brice, Mike Bush, Roger Copeland, Mark Cunningham, Derek Dooley, Ricky Evans, Tony Geter, Greg Glenn, Steve Gordon, Johnny Harper, Kenny Hawkins, Richard Jewell, Mario Johnson, Kent Jordan, Robbie Kamerschen, David Keyes, Bert Lumpkin, Stacey Lundy, Greg McCrary, Greg McElhannon, Scott Mitchell, David Perno, Aderry Pittman, Cal Platt, Pat Poon, Greg Pope, Randy Prater, Chad Rasch, Stacey Samuel, Shun Sims, Byan Skelton, Darrien Smith, Tony Smith, Tommy Stewart, Dedric Thomas, Jeff Wagner, William Watkins, Randy Williams.

1986: Cliff Bowen, Doug Brewster, Robbie Casper, Joe Davis, Trey Davis, Ben Drake, Tracy Dunn, David Eberhart, Pat Hodgson, John Kasay, Chuck Lowe, Jeff Mack, Corey Mapp, Jimmy Maxwell, Alex Nicholson, Camden Pace, Reggie Parrott, Dale Pope, Pat Priester, Bernard Scott, Skipper Strickland, Greg Taylor, Len Thomas, Tracey Woods.

1987: Chip Benton, Carey Best, Eric Bray, Kenneth Brown, Dwayne Carter, Stacey DeFoor, Stuart Dickens, Drew Dukes, Stanley Ezzard, Andre Foster, Milton Gresham, Willie Lester, Gregg Lewis, Andy Mangel, Julian Moses, Rod Platt, Preston Pounds, Chancey Pruitt, J.D. Rasch, Brian Ridley, Chris Scarborough, Bobby Scott, Chuck Smith, Emmitt Smith, Mark Stewart, Warren Sullivan, Whitney Webb, Ralph Whitehead.

1988: George Bailey, Jeff Brock, Kenny Brown, Adrian Jarrell, Roger Johnson, Harry Jones, Chris Lyon, Vince Meglio, Liam Quinlan, Terry Sims, Bobby Stamps, Reginald Taylor, Therron Witcher.

1989: Kevin Bailey, Ted Baker, Kevin Benson, Christopher, Cannon, Baxter Crane, Spencer Crane, Robert Edwards, Uganda Elam, Steve Greer, Iris Hector, Dedrick Hemphill, Geoff Lewis, Clay McElroy, Byron McKinley, Matt Messer, Wesley Middlebrooks, Kevin Morse, Corey Newsom, Robert Pace, Charles Pledger, Kenneth Richardson, Robert Sims, Eric Smith, McAllister Stephens, Brian Tabor.

1990: Johnny Jarrett, Shaun Jones, Mike Jordan, Sam Parker, Mario Payne, Charles Sheats, Tim Stephens, Charlie Taylor, Chad Whittemore, Mike Cox, Henry Delacruz, Clement Doyle, Carlos Freeman, Emory Gilree, Ben Midgette, Lamont Johnson.

1991: Sedric Combs, Dawson Ingram, Jeffery Johnson, Jermaine Barnett, Lacey Degnan, Jay Poindester, Chad Blanchard, Qwe Rucker, Boo Howard, Will Strickland, Lamont Johnson, Clarence Gross, Tyrone Eberhart, Jeff Spratlin, John Thompson, Raushann Jennings, Clay Bryant, Percy Eberhart, Chris Warwick, Corey Wright, Trey Crowley, Charles Smith, Scott Freeney.

1992: Stacy Bailey, Frank Battle, Micah Bennett, Sam Burch, Palmer Bush, Urias Cook, Ben Daniel, Mike Daniels, Antoine Goldwire, Jeff Greer, Kendrick Hall, Mike Harper, Eric Heard, Kevin Johnson, Brian Kenney, Reggie Lewis, Mat McNeil, Godfrey McWhorter, Orlando Muckle, Andy Osbolt, John Dowdy, Kurlen Payton, Ricky Smith, Toron Smith, Brian Ward, Weston Webb, Derrick Jones, Randy Pattnan, Ron Starr, Jon Hicks, Renaldo Billups, Joe Smith.

1993: Mitch Bain, Rivington Kendrick, Billy Merck, Paul Stein, Rick Selleck, Crandall Heard, Mauric Terrell, Tico Rousey, Danny Brooks, Rory Taylor, Perry Johnson, Bill Carter, David Martin, Joel Harber, Al Stephens.

1994: Dan Aldridge, Ethan Amentrout, Stan Baker, Brad Blanchard, Chris Cauthen, Chas Chastain, Garrett Daniel, Andy Dillard, Joey Hall, Brian Harris, Steve Harris, McCullough Hodgson, Chad Hogan, Wes Hogan, Rhett Kopp, Garmel Prophett, Mitch Smith, Reggie Smith, Damille Starr, Arthur Steedman.

1995: Frank Wilson, Mike Lewis, Chaka Walters, Emmitt Smith, Ryan Brinson, Michael Greer, Dicky Sheets, Damien Gary, Tharon Johnson, Cameron Rucker, James Marshall, Zomeak Clark, Clint Chapman, Kofi Attipoe, Dane Cooper, Toron Howard, Dexter Pope, Dwayne Evans, Kinnard Woodall, Akin Miller, Marion Kendricks, Jeff Drake, Lawrence Thomas, Matt McRae, Shane Walls.

Clarke Central Football Scholarships under Henderson

1970s: Kevin Potts (Morris Brown), Bennie Tillman (Memphis State), Tom Gary (Appalachian State), Doug Henson (Georgia Tech), Reggie Bolton (Savannah State), Quinton Bridges (Fort Valley State), George Kesler (Georgia), Bob McLeod (Army), Ricky Smith (Western Carolina), Charles Campbell (Savannah State), Stan Davis (Western Carolina), Jeff Dean (Western Carolina), Jim Bob Harris (Alabama), Karey Johnson (South Carolina), Carey Nelms (UT Chattanooga), Larry Richards (Savannah State), Brent Snyder (Georgia), Bob Weathersby (LSU), Hillary Billups (Morris Brown), Tim Marable (South Carolina), Mac McCoy (Western Carolina).

1980s: Carey Colquitt (Georgia Tech), Charley Dean (Georgia), David Gresham (Virginia), Dwayne Harden (Southern), Joe Marshall (Virginia), Josh Starks (South Carolina), Frank Bush (N.C. State), Rivington Cole (Scottsdale), Robert David (Furman), Eric Griffeth (Scottsdale), Percy Jordan (East Carolina), Darryl Moore (Western Arizona), Damon Pope (East Carolina), Chip Tardy (Georgia). Stuart Ley (Western Carolina), Gerald Mayfield (Troy State), Mark Mitchell (Taft), Ricky Schell (Taft), Dean Shirley (Taft), David Bell (Georgia), Kenny Booker (UT Chattanooga), Mike Cooper (Morehouse), David Dukes (Georgia), Henry Haynes (Georgia Southern), Mark King (Morehouse), Greg Maye (St. Paul's), Bob Tardy (UT Chattanooga), Kevin Terrell (Morehouse), Elliott Walker (Presbyterian), Greg Williams (Georgia Southern), James Barnett (UT Chattanooga), Robin Billups (Western Kentucky), Todd Dunn (Mars Hill), Arnold Grier (Western Kentucky), Dan Henson (Eastern Carolina), Mike Hunter (Western Kentucky), Vic Meglio (Yale), Greg Moses (Clemson), Henry Williams (Georgia), Daryl Brown (UT Chattanooga), Doug Davenport (Marshall), Amp Foster (UT Chattanooga) Willie Green (Ole Miss), Jerry Harris (Marshall), Steve Law (Vanderbilt), Derrick Little (South Carolina), Chip McGinley (Georgia Southern), Chris Morocco (Clemson), Brack Rowe (Tennessee Military), Stan Wilbanks (South Carolina). Clint Bennett (Valdosta State), Roger Copeland (Valdosta State), Derek Dooley (Virginia), Johnny Harper (NE Oklahoma), Richard Jewell (Georgia Southern), Kent Jordan (N.C. State), Robbie Kamerschen (Stanford), David Keyes (Newberry), Scott Mitchell (Scottsdale), Carl Platt (South Carolina), Shaun Sims (Georgia Southern), Dedric Thomas (South Carolina State), Randy Williams (Valdosta State), Doug Brewster (Clemson), Trey Davis (South Carolina State), John Kasay (Georgia), Chuck Lowe (South

Carolina State), Jeff Mack (South Carolina State), Alex Nicholson (N.C. State), Camden Pace (Air Force), Reggie Parrott (Ole Miss), Dale Pope (East Carolina), Bernard Scott (Morris Brown), Skipper Strickland (Presbyterian), Greg Taylor (Morris Brown), Len Thomas (UT Chattanooga), Tracy Woods (Marshall), Kenny Brown (Howard), Milton Gresham (Valdosta State), Willie Lester (South Carolina State), Rod Platt (Indiana), Bobby Scott (Appalachian State), Chuck Smith (Tennessee), Emmitt Smith (Howard), Kenny Brown (South Carolina State), Adrian Jarrell (Notre Dame).

1990s: Kevin Bailey (Tennessee State), Kevin Benson (William Penn), Chris Cannon (NE Oklahoma), Steve Greer (Valdosta State), Matt Messer (Georgia), Kevin Morse (Georgia Southern), Charles Pledger (Georgia), Robert Sims (Howard), McAllister Stephens (Florida A&M), Clement Doyle (Princeton), Carlos Freeman (Georgia Military), Iris Hector (Morris Brown), Mario Payne (Morris Brown), Charles Sheats (Troy State), Charlie Taylor (Morris Brown), Jermaine Barnette (UT-Chattanooga), Scott Freeney (Syracuse), Dawson Ingram (Samford), Lamont Johnson (UT Chattanooga), Que Rucker (Duke), Corey Wright (West Georgia), Frank Battle (UT-Chattanooga), Sam Burch (Princeton), Ben Daniel (Wofford), Antone Goldwire (UT-Chattanooga), Jeff Greer (Valdosta State), Kendrick Hall (Appalachian State), Eric Heard (Hutchinson), Kevin Johnson (Oklahoma/Ohio State), Reggie Lewis (West Georgia), Godfrey McWhorter (Mars Hill), Toron Smith (Jacksonville State/West Georgia), Bill Carter (NE Oklahoma), Rip Kendrick (Middle Georgia), Brad Blanchard (Georgia Military), Chas Chastain (Washington & Lee), Joey Hall (Appalachian State), Reggie Smith (Savannah State), Jeff Drake (Georgia Military), Michael Greer (Georgia), Tharon Johnson (Clark), James Marshall (East Tennessee), Matt McRae (Mississippi State), Emmitt Smith (Grambling).

Clarke Central Players in Pros under Henderson

Doug Brewster (CFL), Frank Bush (Houston Oilers), Bill Carter (Arena Football), Willie Green (Denver Broncos), Joey Hall (Cleveland Browns), Adrian Jarrell (Arena Football), John Kasay (Seattle Seahawks/Carolina Panthers), Chuck Smith (Atlanta Falcons/Carolina Panthers), Cory Hall (Atlanta Falcons), Kevin Johnson (CFL), Percy Jordan (Kansas City Chiefs), Damon Pope (Dallas Cowboys.)